PENGUIN

SELECTED

Thomas Hardy was born in a tiny village near Dorchester on June 2, 1840, the son of a mason and builder. He attended local schools for a few years and at sixteen was apprenticed to a Dorchester architect, John Hicks. In 1862 he went to London to work for the noted architect Arthur Blomfield, and there began seriously to write poetry, but everything he submitted to the magazines was rejected. Five years later, back in Dorset and working for Hicks again, he finished a novel—also rejected but with encouragement to write another. Sent to St. Juliot in Cornwall in 1870 to see to the restoration of its church, he met and fell in love with the rector's sister-in-law, Emma Gifford. He was now determined on a literary career and by the time he and Emma were married in 1874, he had published four novels, including *Far from the Madding Crowd*, which was his first great popular and critical success. In 1885, after living in London and various towns in Dorset, the couple moved into Max Gate, a comfortable house near Dorchester, designed by Hardy and built by his father and brother. There he wrote most of his major novels, *The Mayor of Casterbridge*, *The Woodlanders*, *Tess of the D'Urbervilles*, and *Jude the Obscure*, and several minor ones. In the mid-1890s, tired of writing fiction (which he had done to earn his living and which had by now made him rich), and disgusted with the attacks of the pious and prudish on *Tess* and even more on *Jude*, he returned to his true art and over the next thirty-some years wrote nearly a thousand poems and an epic verse drama, *The Dynasts*. The many years of unhappy and childless marriage and deepening estrangement ended with Emma's sudden death in 1912. Hardy turned his grief and regret into some of the greatest elegies in literature. In 1914 he married his friend and secretary, Florence Dugdale. He was widely regarded as the preeminent man of letters in England and America and received many honors, including the Order of Merit and honorary degrees from Oxford and Cambridge. He died on January 11, 1928. His ashes were interred in Westminster Abbey and his heart in the Stinsford churchyard, a mile or so from where he had been born eighty-eight years before.

Robert Mezey has been poet-in-residence at Pomona College since 1976. A Guggenheim and NEA fellow, he was awarded a prize in poetry by the American Academy of Arts & Letters. *The Lovemaker*, the first of his seven books of verse, won the Lamont Award in 1960; *Evening Wind* appeared in 1987.

# THOMAS HARDY

## SELECTED POEMS

EDITED WITH AN INTRODUCTION
AND NOTES BY ROBERT MEZEY

PENGUIN BOOKS

PENGUIN BOOKS

Published by the Penguin Group

Penguin Group (USA) Inc., 375 Hudson Street, New York, New York 10014, U.S.A.

Penguin Group (Canada), 90 Eglinton Avenue East, Suite 700, Toronto,
Ontario, Canada M4P 2Y3 (a division of Pearson Penguin Canada Inc.)

Penguin Books Ltd, 80 Strand, London WC2R 0RL, England

Penguin Ireland, 25 St Stephen's Green, Dublin 2, Ireland (a division of Penguin Books Ltd)

Penguin Group (Australia), 250 Camberwell Road, Camberwell,
Victoria 3124, Australia (a division of Pearson Australia Group Pty Ltd)

Penguin Books India Pvt Ltd, 11 Community Centre, Panchsheel Park, New Delhi – 110 017, India

Penguin Group (NZ), cnr Airborne and Rosedale Roads,
Albany, Auckland 1310, New Zealand (a division of Pearson New Zealand Ltd)

Penguin Books (South Africa) (Pty) Ltd, 24 Sturdee Avenue,
Rosebank, Johannesburg 2196, South Africa

Penguin Books Ltd, Registered Offices: 80 Strand, London WC2R 0RL, England

This volume first published in Penguin Books 1998

5   7   9   10   8   6

Selection, introduction, and notes copyright © Robert Mezey, 1998
All rights reserved

LIBRARY OF CONGRESS CATALOGING IN PUBLICATION DATA
Hardy, Thomas, 1840–1928.
[Poems. Selections]
Selected poems / Thomas Hardy ; edited with an
introduction and notes by Robert Mezey.
p.    cm.—(Penguin classics)
Includes bibliographical references.
ISBN 0 14 04.3699 5
1. Pastoral poetry, English.    I. Mezey, Robert.
II. Title.    III. Series.
PR4741.M49    1998
821'.8—dc21        98-23288

Printed in the United States of America
Set in Bembo

Except in the United States of America, this book is sold subject to the condition
that it shall not, by way of trade or otherwise, be lent, resold, hired out, or otherwise
circulated without the publisher's prior consent in any form of binding or cover other
than that in which it is published and without a similar condition including
this condition being imposed on the subsequent purchaser.

The scanning, uploading and distribution of this book via the Internet or via any
other means without the permission of the publisher is illegal and punishable by law.
Please purchase only authorized electronic editions, and do not participate in or encourage
electronic piracy of copyrighted materials. Your support of the author's rights is appreciated.

for Don and Jean

*The thrushes sing as the sun is going*

# CONTENTS

Introduction . . . . . . . . . . . . . . . . . . . . . . . . . . . . . . . . . . . xv
Chronology. . . . . . . . . . . . . . . . . . . . . . . . . . . . . . . . . . . xxxix
Suggestions for Further Reading . . . . . . . . . . . . . . . . . . lv
Note on the Selection . . . . . . . . . . . . . . . . . . . . . . . . lvii

Domicilium. . . . . . . . . . . . . . . . . . . . . . . . . . . . . . . . . . . . .1

## From WESSEX POEMS AND OTHER VERSES

Hap . . . . . . . . . . . . . . . . . . . . . . . . . . . . . . . . . . . . . . . . . . .5
Neutral Tones . . . . . . . . . . . . . . . . . . . . . . . . . . . . . . . . . . .5
She, to Him II. . . . . . . . . . . . . . . . . . . . . . . . . . . . . . . . . . .6
Friends Beyond . . . . . . . . . . . . . . . . . . . . . . . . . . . . . . . . .7
Nature's Questioning . . . . . . . . . . . . . . . . . . . . . . . . . . . . .9
In a Eweleaze near Weatherbury . . . . . . . . . . . . . . . . . .10
"I Look Into My Glass" . . . . . . . . . . . . . . . . . . . . . . . . .11

## From POEMS OF THE PAST AND THE PRESENT

Embarcation . . . . . . . . . . . . . . . . . . . . . . . . . . . . . . . . . . .15
Drummer Hodge . . . . . . . . . . . . . . . . . . . . . . . . . . . . . . .15
The Souls of the Slain . . . . . . . . . . . . . . . . . . . . . . . . . . .16
Rome: At the Pyramid of Cestius Near the Graves of
    Shelley and Keats . . . . . . . . . . . . . . . . . . . . . . . . . . .21
Zermatt: To the Matterhorn . . . . . . . . . . . . . . . . . . . . .22
To an Unborn Pauper Child. . . . . . . . . . . . . . . . . . . . . .22
To Lizbie Browne . . . . . . . . . . . . . . . . . . . . . . . . . . . . . .24
"I Need Not Go" . . . . . . . . . . . . . . . . . . . . . . . . . . . . . .27
At a Hasty Wedding. . . . . . . . . . . . . . . . . . . . . . . . . . . .28
His Immortality . . . . . . . . . . . . . . . . . . . . . . . . . . . . . . .28

Wives in the Sere. . . . . . . . . . . . . . . . . . . . . . . . . . . . . . .29
An August Midnight . . . . . . . . . . . . . . . . . . . . . . . . . . . .30
Winter in Durnover Field. . . . . . . . . . . . . . . . . . . . . . . .31
The Last Chrysanthemum. . . . . . . . . . . . . . . . . . . . . . .32
The Darkling Thrush . . . . . . . . . . . . . . . . . . . . . . . . . . .33
Mad Judy . . . . . . . . . . . . . . . . . . . . . . . . . . . . . . . . . . . .34
The Ruined Maid . . . . . . . . . . . . . . . . . . . . . . . . . . . . . .35
The Respectable Burgher on "The Higher Criticism" . . . .36
The Self-Unseeing . . . . . . . . . . . . . . . . . . . . . . . . . . . . .37
In Tenebris I. . . . . . . . . . . . . . . . . . . . . . . . . . . . . . . . . .38

## From TIME'S LAUGHINGSTOCKS AND OTHER VERSES

A Trampwoman's Tragedy . . . . . . . . . . . . . . . . . . . . . . .41
The House of Hospitalities . . . . . . . . . . . . . . . . . . . . . .45
The Rejected Member's Wife . . . . . . . . . . . . . . . . . . . . .46
Shut Out That Moon. . . . . . . . . . . . . . . . . . . . . . . . . . .47
The Division. . . . . . . . . . . . . . . . . . . . . . . . . . . . . . . . . .48
"I Say I'll Seek Her" . . . . . . . . . . . . . . . . . . . . . . . . . . .48
"In the Night She Came". . . . . . . . . . . . . . . . . . . . . . . .49
The Night of the Dance. . . . . . . . . . . . . . . . . . . . . . . . .50

**At Casterbridge Fair**
   The Ballad-Singer. . . . . . . . . . . . . . . . . . . . . . . . . . . .51
   Former Beauties . . . . . . . . . . . . . . . . . . . . . . . . . . . . .51
   After the Club-Dance . . . . . . . . . . . . . . . . . . . . . . . . .52
   The Market-Girl . . . . . . . . . . . . . . . . . . . . . . . . . . . .52
   The Inquiry. . . . . . . . . . . . . . . . . . . . . . . . . . . . . . . .53
   A Wife Waits. . . . . . . . . . . . . . . . . . . . . . . . . . . . . . .54
   After the Fair . . . . . . . . . . . . . . . . . . . . . . . . . . . . . . .54
To Carrey Clavel. . . . . . . . . . . . . . . . . . . . . . . . . . . . . .55
The Orphaned Old Maid . . . . . . . . . . . . . . . . . . . . . . .56
Rose-Ann. . . . . . . . . . . . . . . . . . . . . . . . . . . . . . . . . . . .56
The Homecoming . . . . . . . . . . . . . . . . . . . . . . . . . . . .57
A Church Romance. . . . . . . . . . . . . . . . . . . . . . . . . . . .59
After the Last Breath . . . . . . . . . . . . . . . . . . . . . . . . . .60

One We Knew . . . . . . . . . . . . . . . . . . . . . . . . . . . . . 61
She Hears the Storm . . . . . . . . . . . . . . . . . . . . . . . . 62
The Man He Killed . . . . . . . . . . . . . . . . . . . . . . . . . 63
One Ralph Blossom Soliloquizes . . . . . . . . . . . . . . . . . 64

**From SATIRES OF CIRCUMSTANCE, LYRICS
  AND REVERIES**

Channel Firing. . . . . . . . . . . . . . . . . . . . . . . . . . . . . 69
The Convergence of the Twain. . . . . . . . . . . . . . . . . . 70
"My Spirit Will Not Haunt the Mound" . . . . . . . . . . . 72
Wessex Heights . . . . . . . . . . . . . . . . . . . . . . . . . . . . 73
The Schreckhorn . . . . . . . . . . . . . . . . . . . . . . . . . . . 75
"Ah, Are You Digging on My Grave?" . . . . . . . . . . . . 75
Before and After Summer . . . . . . . . . . . . . . . . . . . . . 77
At Day-Close in November . . . . . . . . . . . . . . . . . . . 78
**Poems of 1912–13**
  The Going. . . . . . . . . . . . . . . . . . . . . . . . . . . . . . 79
  Your Last Drive . . . . . . . . . . . . . . . . . . . . . . . . . 80
  The Walk . . . . . . . . . . . . . . . . . . . . . . . . . . . . . . 81
  Rain on a Grave . . . . . . . . . . . . . . . . . . . . . . . . . 82
  Without Ceremony . . . . . . . . . . . . . . . . . . . . . . . 83
  Lament . . . . . . . . . . . . . . . . . . . . . . . . . . . . . . . 84
  The Haunter . . . . . . . . . . . . . . . . . . . . . . . . . . . . 85
  The Voice. . . . . . . . . . . . . . . . . . . . . . . . . . . . . . 86
  His Visitor. . . . . . . . . . . . . . . . . . . . . . . . . . . . . 87
  After a Journey. . . . . . . . . . . . . . . . . . . . . . . . . . 88
  At Castle Boterel . . . . . . . . . . . . . . . . . . . . . . . . 89
"She Charged Me" . . . . . . . . . . . . . . . . . . . . . . . . . 91
The Moon Looks In . . . . . . . . . . . . . . . . . . . . . . . . 91
In the Days of Crinoline. . . . . . . . . . . . . . . . . . . . . . 92
The Workbox . . . . . . . . . . . . . . . . . . . . . . . . . . . . . 93
Exeunt Omnes. . . . . . . . . . . . . . . . . . . . . . . . . . . . . 95
**Satires of Circumstance in Fifteen Glimpses**
  At Tea . . . . . . . . . . . . . . . . . . . . . . . . . . . . . . . . 96
  In Church . . . . . . . . . . . . . . . . . . . . . . . . . . . . . 96

By Her Aunt's Grave . . . . . . . . . . . . . . . . . . . . . . . . . . 97
In the Room of the Bride-Elect. . . . . . . . . . . . . . . . . . 97
At a Watering-Place . . . . . . . . . . . . . . . . . . . . . . . . . . 98
In the Cemetery. . . . . . . . . . . . . . . . . . . . . . . . . . . . . 98
Outside the Window . . . . . . . . . . . . . . . . . . . . . . . . . 99
In the Study. . . . . . . . . . . . . . . . . . . . . . . . . . . . . . . . 99
At the Altar-Rail . . . . . . . . . . . . . . . . . . . . . . . . . . 100
In the Nuptial Chamber . . . . . . . . . . . . . . . . . . . . . 101
In the Restaurant . . . . . . . . . . . . . . . . . . . . . . . . . . 101
At the Draper's. . . . . . . . . . . . . . . . . . . . . . . . . . . . 102
On the Death-Bed . . . . . . . . . . . . . . . . . . . . . . . . . 102
Over the Coffin. . . . . . . . . . . . . . . . . . . . . . . . . . . . 103
In the Moonlight . . . . . . . . . . . . . . . . . . . . . . . . . . 104

## From MOMENTS OF VISION AND
## MISCELLANEOUS VERSES

"We Sat at the Window" . . . . . . . . . . . . . . . . . . . . . 107
Afternoon Service at Mellstock . . . . . . . . . . . . . . . . . 107
At the Word "Farewell" . . . . . . . . . . . . . . . . . . . . . . 108
Heredity . . . . . . . . . . . . . . . . . . . . . . . . . . . . . . . . . 109
Near Lanivet, 1872. . . . . . . . . . . . . . . . . . . . . . . . . 109
To the Moon . . . . . . . . . . . . . . . . . . . . . . . . . . . . . 111
Timing Her. . . . . . . . . . . . . . . . . . . . . . . . . . . . . . . 112
The Blinded Bird. . . . . . . . . . . . . . . . . . . . . . . . . . 114
"The Wind Blew Words". . . . . . . . . . . . . . . . . . . . . 115
To My Father's Violin . . . . . . . . . . . . . . . . . . . . . . 116
The Pedigree. . . . . . . . . . . . . . . . . . . . . . . . . . . . . . 117
Where They Lived. . . . . . . . . . . . . . . . . . . . . . . . . . 119
"Something Tapped" . . . . . . . . . . . . . . . . . . . . . . . . 120
The Oxen. . . . . . . . . . . . . . . . . . . . . . . . . . . . . . . . 120
The Photograph. . . . . . . . . . . . . . . . . . . . . . . . . . . 121
An Anniversary . . . . . . . . . . . . . . . . . . . . . . . . . . . 122
Transformations . . . . . . . . . . . . . . . . . . . . . . . . . . . 123
The Last Signal . . . . . . . . . . . . . . . . . . . . . . . . . . . 123
Great Things . . . . . . . . . . . . . . . . . . . . . . . . . . . . . 124

At Middle-Field Gate in February . . . . . . . . . . . . . . . . . 125
On Sturminster Foot-Bridge . . . . . . . . . . . . . . . . . . . . 126
Old Furniture . . . . . . . . . . . . . . . . . . . . . . . . . . . . 126
A Thought in Two Moods . . . . . . . . . . . . . . . . . . . . . 128
Logs on the Hearth . . . . . . . . . . . . . . . . . . . . . . . . . 128
The Caged Goldfinch . . . . . . . . . . . . . . . . . . . . . . . . 129
The Ballet . . . . . . . . . . . . . . . . . . . . . . . . . . . . . . 129
The Five Students . . . . . . . . . . . . . . . . . . . . . . . . . . 130
During Wind and Rain . . . . . . . . . . . . . . . . . . . . . . . 131
He Prefers Her Earthly . . . . . . . . . . . . . . . . . . . . . . . 132
A Backward Spring . . . . . . . . . . . . . . . . . . . . . . . . . 133
"Who's in the Next Room?" . . . . . . . . . . . . . . . . . . . . 133
At a Country Fair . . . . . . . . . . . . . . . . . . . . . . . . . . 134
Jubilate . . . . . . . . . . . . . . . . . . . . . . . . . . . . . . . . 135
Midnight on the Great Western . . . . . . . . . . . . . . . . . . 136
The Shadow on the Stone . . . . . . . . . . . . . . . . . . . . . 137
In the Garden . . . . . . . . . . . . . . . . . . . . . . . . . . . . 138
An Upbraiding . . . . . . . . . . . . . . . . . . . . . . . . . . . . 138
The Choirmaster's Burial . . . . . . . . . . . . . . . . . . . . . 139
In Time of "The Breaking of Nations" . . . . . . . . . . . . . 141
Afterwards . . . . . . . . . . . . . . . . . . . . . . . . . . . . . . 142

## From LATE LYRICS AND EARLIER

Weathers . . . . . . . . . . . . . . . . . . . . . . . . . . . . . . . 145
The Garden Seat . . . . . . . . . . . . . . . . . . . . . . . . . . . 145
"According to the Mighty Working" . . . . . . . . . . . . . . . 146
Going and Staying . . . . . . . . . . . . . . . . . . . . . . . . . . 147
The Contretemps . . . . . . . . . . . . . . . . . . . . . . . . . . 148
A Night in November . . . . . . . . . . . . . . . . . . . . . . . . 150
The Fallow Deer at the Lonely House . . . . . . . . . . . . . . 150
On the Tune Called the Old-Hundred-and-Fourth . . . . . 151
Voices from Things Growing in a Churchyard . . . . . . . . 152
A Two-Years' Idyll . . . . . . . . . . . . . . . . . . . . . . . . . 154
Fetching Her . . . . . . . . . . . . . . . . . . . . . . . . . . . . . 155
A Procession of Dead Days . . . . . . . . . . . . . . . . . . . . 156

In the Small Hours. . . . . . . . . . . . . . . . . . . . . . . . . 157
The Dream Is—Which? . . . . . . . . . . . . . . . . . . . . . 158
Lonely Days . . . . . . . . . . . . . . . . . . . . . . . . . . . . 159
The Marble Tablet. . . . . . . . . . . . . . . . . . . . . . . . . 160
The Master and the Leaves . . . . . . . . . . . . . . . . . . . 161
Last Words to a Dumb Friend. . . . . . . . . . . . . . . . . 162
An Ancient to Ancients . . . . . . . . . . . . . . . . . . . . . 164

## From HUMAN SHOWS, FAR PHANTASIES, SONGS AND TRIFLES

Waiting Both. . . . . . . . . . . . . . . . . . . . . . . . . . . . 169
A Bird-Scene at a Rural Dwelling . . . . . . . . . . . . . . . 169
Coming Up Oxford Street: Evening. . . . . . . . . . . . . . 170
When Dead. . . . . . . . . . . . . . . . . . . . . . . . . . . . . 170
Ten Years Since. . . . . . . . . . . . . . . . . . . . . . . . . . 171
Life and Death at Sunrise . . . . . . . . . . . . . . . . . . . 172
A Sheep Fair . . . . . . . . . . . . . . . . . . . . . . . . . . . . 173
The Calf. . . . . . . . . . . . . . . . . . . . . . . . . . . . . . . 174
Snow in the Suburbs . . . . . . . . . . . . . . . . . . . . . . 175
Ice on the Highway . . . . . . . . . . . . . . . . . . . . . . . 176
No Buyers . . . . . . . . . . . . . . . . . . . . . . . . . . . . . 176
One Who Married Above Him. . . . . . . . . . . . . . . . . 177
Last Love-Word. . . . . . . . . . . . . . . . . . . . . . . . . . 179
Nobody Comes. . . . . . . . . . . . . . . . . . . . . . . . . . . 180
When Oats Were Reaped. . . . . . . . . . . . . . . . . . . . . 180
The Harbour Bridge. . . . . . . . . . . . . . . . . . . . . . . . 181
The Missed Train. . . . . . . . . . . . . . . . . . . . . . . . . 182
Retty's Phases . . . . . . . . . . . . . . . . . . . . . . . . . . . 183
The Sundial on a Wet Day. . . . . . . . . . . . . . . . . . . 184
Shortening Days at the Homestead. . . . . . . . . . . . . . . 185
A Hurried Meeting . . . . . . . . . . . . . . . . . . . . . . . . 186
A Leaving. . . . . . . . . . . . . . . . . . . . . . . . . . . . . . 188

## From WINTER WORDS IN VARIOUS MOODS AND METRES

Proud Songsters . . . . . . . . . . . . . . . . . . . . . . . . . . . . . . 191
"I Am the One" . . . . . . . . . . . . . . . . . . . . . . . . . . . . . . 191
Expectation and Experience. . . . . . . . . . . . . . . . . . . . . 192
Throwing a Tree . . . . . . . . . . . . . . . . . . . . . . . . . . . . . . 193
Lying Awake. . . . . . . . . . . . . . . . . . . . . . . . . . . . . . . . 194
Henley Regatta . . . . . . . . . . . . . . . . . . . . . . . . . . . . . . 194
"A Gentleman's Second-Hand Suit" . . . . . . . . . . . . . . . 195
A Forgotten Miniature . . . . . . . . . . . . . . . . . . . . . . . . 196


Appendix: Hardy's Notes and Remarks . . . . . . . . . . . . 197
Notes . . . . . . . . . . . . . . . . . . . . . . . . . . . . . . . . . . . . 205
Index of Titles and First Lines . . . . . . . . . . . . . . . . . . 245

# INTRODUCTION

"This curious and wearisome volume, these many slovenly, slip-shod, uncouth verses, stilted in sentiment, poorly conceived and worse wrought. . . . It is impossible to understand why the bulk of this volume was published at all—why he did not himself burn the verse, lest it should fall into the hands of an indiscreet literary executor, and mar his fame when he was dead." Thus *The Saturday Review*, rendering judgment on *Wessex Poems*, Hardy's first book of verse, published in 1898 when he was almost sixty years old. Other reviewers were equally solicitous, worried lest this grand old man of letters diminish his reputation with these clumsy and amateurish efforts, "a dubious experiment for a proseman to sit in the Siege Perilous of poetry." There were similar brutalities from other periodicals. Most were simply puzzled, wondering why this distinguished and popular novelist should start fooling around with poetry at his age. The *Atheneum* found it "difficult to say the proper word," but then found it: "We do not conceal our opinion that Mr. Hardy's success in poetry is of a very narrow range." The story was much the same in America: "We are unable to find any beauty of poetic expression," "faulty rhymes and rough accents," "lyrical charm is almost completely absent," and so on. And there were complaints about the dark or lurid atmosphere of the poems, the profound melancholy, the pessimism; Lytton Strachey no doubt spoke for many when he wrote, some years later, "the gloom is not even relieved by a little elegance of diction" (although he came to admire the poems and say some fine things about them). In all fairness, it must be said that there were also many good and courteous reviews, properly deferential to one of the most eminent writers in the English-speaking world; and through the years, admirers and advocates have not been lacking. Nevertheless, the disparagements continued, and although diminished, continue to this day. Sometimes they have been decidedly intemperate. In 1940, R. P. Blackmur damaged Hardy's reputation in an influential essay, at once fatuous and savage, in which he charged Hardy with lacking a tradition, an education, and a sense of craft; said he had an authoritarian and totalitarian mind that must eventually resort to violence; that he was unaware of the nature of poetic work, incapable of choice, cynical and meretricious, unable to discriminate between good and evil, and had no idea what he was doing; and concluded that his poetry is a general failure and that his few good poems must be accidents! This from a man who published one slim volume of poems, all of them bad. F. R. Leavis was not much friendlier and almost as obtuse. In the 1960s, Philip Larkin, James Wright, and others wondered why Hardy had attracted so few good critics, and although the situation has changed somewhat in the last few decades, his poetic stock still fluctuates erratically. Well, as he himself wrote, criticism is so easy, and art so hard.

But criticism isn't really all that easy, or there would be more good criticism. Even some of Hardy's admirers have not known quite how to deal with him. As Donald Davie put it, "Hardy's poetry is a body of writing before which one honest critic after another has by his own confession retired, baffled and defeated," and he quotes Irving Howe:

> Any critic can, and often does, see all that is wrong with Hardy's poetry, but whatever it was that makes for his strange greatness is much harder to describe. Can there ever have been a critic of Hardy who, before poems like "The Going" and "During Wind and Rain," did not feel the grating inadequacy of verbal analysis, and the need to resort to such treacherous terms as "honesty," "sincerity," and even "wisdom"?

And now he has begun to fall into the hands of the so-called postmodernists. One recent editor of a Selected Poems accuses Hardy of being quietist and apolitical and "imbricated, personally and professionally, by patriarchal ideology," taxes him with prurience and "the male gaze" and with taking up poetry out of petit-bourgeois snobbery, and does the obligatory "problematizing" and "deconstructing," but coyly suggests that he still manages to like Hardy's poems! In fact, he likes them so well that in a selection of nearly 200 poems he leaves out fifty or sixty of the most beautiful and includes at least a score that only a Hardy lover could love. With such friends, who needs enemies?

There is an amusing passage in *Good-bye to All That* (1929) in which Robert Graves, during a visit to Max Gate, asks Hardy about the critics and reports his response:

> He regarded professional critics as parasites, no less noxious than autograph hunters, wished the world rid of them, and also regretted having listened to them as a young man; on their advice he had cut out from his early poems dialect-words which possessed no ordinary English equivalents. And still the critics were plaguing him. One of them complained of a line: "his shape smalled in the distance." Now, what in the world else could he have written? Hardy then laughed a little. Once or twice recently he had looked up a word in the dictionary for fear of being again accused of coining, and found it there right enough —only to read on and discover that the sole authority quoted was himself in a half-forgotten novel.

But it is important to remember that the instability of Hardy's poetic reputation and the patronizing or carping criticism have been the work of professional critics and academics. The common readers of poetry have paid little attention to what the "licensed tasters" say; they have gone on reading and enjoying the poems for a century. His poetry has never been out of print; indeed, the collected poems went through so many reprintings that by the 1970s the plates had deteriorated to the point that the texts were barely legible, and in 1976 James Gibson produced a new edition much superior to the old one. And Hardy's fellow poets have admired and praised him from the beginning. The outstanding poets who have been his champions, and in many of whom one can see his influence writ large or small, are legion and of an astonishing variety. Even a fairly short list would have to include A. E. Housman, W. B. Yeats, Rudyard Kipling, E. A. Robinson, Robert Frost, Ezra Pound, Siegfried Sassoon, Robinson Jeffers, John Crowe Ransom, Robert Graves, Louise Bogan, Yvor Winters, C. Day Lewis, Robert Penn Warren, W. H. Auden, Dylan Thomas, Robert Lowell, Philip Larkin, Edgar Bowers, David Ferry, Donald Justice, James Wright, John Hollander, Miller Williams—one could go on and on—and most of these have regarded Hardy as far and away the greatest English poet of his era or of the century. It is surely a matter for wonderment when minds as independent and dissimilar as those of Winters, Pound, Ransom, Jeffers, and Larkin strongly agree about anything. Winters went even further: "There is probably not another master of English verse and of the English language as rich and profound this side of Shakespeare." I would agree. Among the moderns, his only peer is Frost and, perhaps, Yeats.

A knowledgeable reader would not be taken aback by that long list of Hardy admirers; some of them—Ransom, Auden, and Larkin, among others—clearly took him for their master. The only name that might perhaps surprise us is Ezra Pound, highest of High Modernists, and we might be still more surprised by how lavish Pound's praise was. Like almost everyone else, I vaguely knew that Pound respected him, and I recalled his having said, "Nobody has taught me anything about writing since Thomas Hardy died," and also "Now *there* is clarity. There is the harvest of having written twenty novels first." (Fourteen,

actually.) I asked my poet and scholar friends, many of whom
have read more widely than I, and only two of them had ever
come across Pound's writing on Hardy beyond those two oft-
quoted remarks; nor did I know of it myself until three or four
years ago. Some excerpts from *Guide to Kulchur* (1938):

> . . . Expression coterminous with the matter. Nothing
> for disciples' exploitation. When we, if we live long
> enough, come to estimate the "poetry of the period,"
> against Hardy's 600 pages we will put what?
>     . . . If I have, a few pages back, set a measure for
> music, I set another for poetry. No man can read
> Hardy's poems collected but that his own life, and
> forgotten moments of it, will come back to him, a
> flash here and an hour there. Have you a better test
> of true poetry?
>     . . . No thoughtful writer can read this book of
> Hardy's without throwing his own work (in imagi-
> nation) into the test-tube and hunting it for fustian,
> for the foolish word, for the word upholstered.
>     Here also are poems that his French contemporar-
> ies, and those older a bit than he was—the best of
> them—could have respected. There is a flood of life
> caught in this crystal. . . .

And some from the anthology *Confucius to Cummings* (1964):

> Clear page or palimpsest, Hardy registered an age.
> Of conventional mind, apparently, but of a very par-
> ticular sensibility. . . .
>     . . . Contemporary for a long time with Browning
> on whom he improves, at his, Hardy's, best, taking
> over the marrow of the tradition. . . .
>     . . . No one trying to learn writing in regular,
> formed verse can learn better than in observing what

Thomas Hardy accepted from Browning and what he pruned away. . . .

. . . The chronology in most of his collections is, he admits, jumbled. What I learned . . . was the degree in which he would have had his mind on the SUBJECT MATTER, and how little he cared about manner, which does not in the least mean that he did not care about it or had not a definite aim. Also, having printed only four poems up to the age of fifty-eight, the lifetime spent in novel-writing gave him a magnificent tool kit, and if you have the sense to read without jingling, there is emphasis as it falls in the natural phrasing. . . .

Nobody, on occasion, ever used rhyme with less insult to statement, but the road to this accomplishment left a number of botches, and a lot of words he would not have used in writing prose.

. . . the poems of 1912–13 lift him to his apex, sixteen poems from "The Going" to "At Castle Boterel," all good, and enough for a lifetime. . . .

It is usually fruitless to ask *what if;* still, I cannot but wonder if modern poetry might not have taken a somewhat different course had Pound paid this homage in the early twenties and had it been as widely known as *Make It New* or other of Pound's influential essays of the time.

The only poet of stature to attack Hardy's work was T. S. Eliot, and he expressed his animadversion in very peculiar terms. He called Hardy "a powerful personality uncurbed by any institutional attachment or by submission to any objective beliefs. . . ." At the time Eliot wrote this, he was a devout Anglo-Catholic, and it sounds as if he regarded Hardy as quite literally a heretic, one who chooses to think for himself—converts are very passionate about their own "objective beliefs," especially in confronting an apostate. He went on to censure Hardy for being "indifferent even to the precepts of good writing: he wrote sometimes overpoweringly well, but always very carelessly; at times his style touches sublimity without ever having passed through the stage of being good." This strikes me as hilarious—Eliot, surely an intelligent and sensitive reader, is obviously moved by the power of Hardy's writing but obscurely offended by the *way* it moves him. It doesn't seem to have occurred to him, as it has to other readers, that the intermittent carelessness was part of the power, and that it was for the most part deliberate: Hardy was not indifferent to his *own* precepts of good writing. And what law says that you have to be good before you can hope to be sublime? Life is so unfair. But Eliot at least had the sense to realize that his antipathy was too personal, too temperamental, to be of much use to anyone, and he admitted that it might have been better not to write about Hardy at all. Still, he let it stand. Odd.

*    *    *    *

Having tried without success to market his early verse, Hardy began around 1870 to write fiction. He did not wish to spend the rest of his life as an architect, and he needed an income sufficient to marry on. Bent on achieving commercial success, he was prepared to sacrifice a great deal to that end, readily agreeing to revisions and cuts suggested by the cautious editors of popular magazines. In his old age, after he had stopped writing fiction, he continually downplayed it. "I was forced to manufacture my novels," he said, "circumstances compelled me to turn them out." And to Vere Collins: "I never cared very much about writing novels. And I should not have—[pause]. Besides, I had written quite enough novels." (I suspect that what he was going to say before he paused, perhaps thinking better of it, was that if he could only have earned his livelihood as a poet, he would never have written a single novel.) But during the years that he was writing them, he took them seriously enough, and he had certain conscious and explicit aims, perhaps the most urgent of which was to record as fully and accurately as he could the culture of his native village and region, a way of life that had gone on virtually unchanged since the Middle Ages but was now rapidly disappearing in his own lifetime. He knew that the immense changes of the latter half of the nineteenth century had in many ways improved the lives of rural people and was glad for that, but he could not help regretting what had been lost, and elegizing it in novels, in poems, and in conversation:

> For one thing, village tradition—a vast mass of un-written folk-lore, local chronicle, local topography and nomenclature—is absolutely sinking, has nearly sunk, into eternal oblivion. I cannot recall a single instance of a labourer who still lives on the farm where he was born, and I can only recall a few who have been five years on their present farms. Thus you see, there being no continuity of environment in their lives, there is no continuity of information, the names, stories, and relics of one place being speedily forgotten under the incoming facts of the next. For example, if you ask one of the workfolk (they always used to be called "workfolk" hereabout—"labourers" is an imported word) the names of surrounding hills, streams; the character and circumstances of people buried in particular graves; at what spots parish per-sonages lie interred; questions on local fairies, ghosts, herbs, etc., they can give no answer: yet I can rec-ollect the time when the places of burial even of the poor and tombless were all remembered, and the his-tory of the parish and squire's family for 150 years back known. Such and such ballads appertained to such and such a locality, ghost tales were attached to particular sites, and nooks wherein wild herbs grew for the cure of divers maladies were pointed out readily.

And he was enough of a Victorian and a moralist to want to do good: "What are my books but one plea against 'man's in-

humanity to man'—to woman—and to the lower animals?"
Nor could he resist the demands of his imagination. He did not
cease being a poet while he was writing his novels, as any reader
knows; many of the scenes we remember most vividly are the
most poetic, like Troy's sword exercise in the hollow amid the
ferns in *Far from the Madding Crowd* or the brooding meditation
on Egdon Heath that opens *The Return of the Native*. Coventry
Patmore, like many other poets, loved *Under the Greenwood Tree*,
but said he wished it had been written in verse. One might say
that Hardy became a great novelist in spite of himself.

Most novelists have written poems at one time or another,
but Hardy is the only writer in English literature, the only one
I can think of, who can be said to have achieved greatness in
both fiction and poetry. It is a very rare thing. Swift, Meredith,
and Kipling are his only possible rivals, but as poets, though
they are very good, none of them is in Hardy's class. The only
other names that occur to me are Emily Brontë and Robert
Louis Stevenson, both excellent novelists, but very minor poets.

"To be known as a good hand at a serial" was an ambition
he expressed more than once, and it is certainly modest—char-
acteristically so: everyone attested to his humility and self-
effacement. His ambition as a poet may sound equally modest,
to have "a few poems in a good anthology, like Palgrave's,"
but that is in fact a large hope. Frost said, "The utmost of
ambition is to lodge a few poems where they will be hard to
get rid of." And like Frost, Hardy has lodged more than a few.

*       *       *       *

What is it that has given some of Hardy's critics so much trouble
and incited them to deprecate his poetry? Perhaps its very ac-
cessibility; as Larkin put it, "modern criticism thrives on the
difficult—either on explaining the difficult or explaining that
what seemed straightforward is in fact difficult—and Hardy is
simple; his work contains little in thought or reference that
needs elucidation, his language is unambiguous, his themes eas-
ily comprehensible." In some quarters, the kiss of death. But he

is most commonly abused for his "pessimism," his ideas, and the awkwardness of his verse and his diction. The charge of pessimism was the one that seems most to have set his teeth on edge, and one can see why. It is, after all, a rather crude category, "a mere nickname," as he said, "with no sense in it," and he thought, quite rightly, that it was an easy way for people to ignore or ward off those elements in his work that were, and are, disturbing. He tried more than once to explain himself: "Differing natures find their tongue in the presence of differing spectacles. Some natures become vocal at tragedy, some are made vocal by comedy, and it seems to me that to whichever aspects of life a writer's instinct for expression the more readily responds, to that he should allow it to respond." He might have said, with Fulke Greville, that he "chose not to write to them on whose foot the black ox had not already trod, as the proverb is, but to those that are weather-beaten in the sea of this world." But no, that wouldn't have helped; it was all to no avail, and he might have done best to say nothing. Such accusations in the heyday of Queen Victoria are understandable, but that they are still sometimes heard today is absurd. Compared to James Thomson, Housman, Kees, Larkin, or Plath, not to mention Beckett or Celine, Hardy seems almost upbeat. And in fact there is a lot of humor in his work, and joy too, as more than one reader has noticed. Pound said that "Hardy stood for the joie de vivre," and Padraic Colum that "the substance of his poetry comes from his love of life," and made a long list of the things that Hardy enjoyed and loved. And Larkin, while conceding that "the dominant emotion in Hardy is sadness," did not fail to register his "buoyancy and relish and toughness."

As Nietzsche said, "All good things are powerful stimulants to life, even a good book which is written *against* life." And there is this too, that with any good artist, the blackest and most turbulent feelings—grief, indignation, despair—are somehow inseparable from the pleasure of making, the lift, the exaltation that the work is striving toward. Think of Goya's morbid and violent etchings, the nightmarish scenes of rapine, slaughter, dismemberment: there is a gusto to it, is there not?—the conveyed joy of the artist delighting in the exercise of his powers. Florence, Hardy's second wife, in a letter to a friend: "Hardy is now, this afternoon, writing a poem with great spirit: always a sign of well-being with him. Needless to say, it is an intensely dismal poem."

Hardy considered himself and has generally been considered an agnostic, but what he really is is a Christian who is simply no longer able to believe in Christian doctrine and mythology. His piety goes far beyond being "churchy," as he once described himself. Even his so-called pessimism is not so very different from the Christian vision of this world as seen through a glass darkly, a vale of tears from which death is an escape, a liberation, a victory. What he believed, or sometimes believed, or thought he believed, is that it is our tragedy to be burdened by consciousness—"Thought is a disease of the flesh," he wrote once—and by a seemingly infinite capacity for suffering in a universe utterly indifferent to our desires, to our existence: "The world does not despise us; it only neglects us." He was one of those men who never get over the discovery of how much pain there is in the world, not merely their own pain but that of other creatures, which they seem to feel as keenly as their own; he remained all his life at the mercy of what James Wright calls his "defenseless compassion." No wonder he often thought of death as a friend and was more than half in love with it. How happy some of his ghosts are! If they are not in a state of bliss, they are certainly at peace: they murmur contentedly, they dance, they fervently hope there will be no resurrection. There is a curious mixture of gratitude and regret in the story he tells of being reclaimed from death by a midwife ("Lizzie D . . .") attending at his birth. The doctor had laid him aside as stillborn, but she insisted he was alive, and she proved it. This is family lore and may well be apocryphal, but it was true for him, and there seems to me a subterranean connection between that near-miss and his lifelong obsession with a spectral existence, sleeping the long sleep, changing into grass or flowers—all the many forms that death took in his imagination. If I may be forgiven for quoting myself, I have said this better in verse than I can do in prose:

> *Thrown away at birth, he was recovered,*
> *Plucked from the swaddling-shroud, and chafed and slapped,*
> *The crone implacable. At last he shivered,*
> *Drew the first breath, and howled, and lay there, trapped*
> *In a world from which there is but one escape*
> *And that forestalled now almost ninety years.*
> *In such a scene as he himself might shape,*
> *The maker of a thousand songs appears.*
>
> *From this it follows, all the ironies*
> *Life plays on one whose fate it is to follow*
> *The way of things, the suffering one sees,*
> *The many cups of bitterness he must swallow*
> *Before he is permitted to be gone*
> *Where he was headed in that early dawn.*

I have been thinking about the account that Michael Millgate, Hardy's magisterial biographer, gives of his death, and trying to imagine it. How strange to think that this man, who wrote about death continually, who was preoccupied with it for some eighty years, who had witnessed at least two hangings and held up a candle at an autopsy and supervised the digging up of corpses to remove them to another graveyard, who had meditated on death, studied it, felt its attraction, should at the very moment of death raise his head from the pillow, eyes wide open, and clasping his sister-in-law's hand, cry out, "Eva, what *is* this?"

*        *        *        *

Virginia Woolf, reviewing one of Hardy's novels:

> Nothing is more necessary in reading an imaginative
> writer, than to keep the right distance above his page.
> Nothing is easier, especially with a writer of marked
> idiosyncracy, than to fasten on opinions, convict him
> of a creed, tether him to a consistent point of view.

And what she warned against is exactly what happened. He
was attacked for opinions that were regarded by many as blas-
phemous and immoral, a threat against Victorian social arrange-
ments, against the class system, the subjection of women,
dogmas religious and secular—he was convicted of a creed. He
has been faulted by later critics for the ubiquity and rigidity of
his ideas and for imposing them rather mechanically on his po-
ems. We must concede that some of the less memorable poems
seem to have been written in order to demonstrate yet again
the cruelty and indifference of fate, the blindness of what,
among other things, he liked to call the Immanent Will; and it
must be admitted that he did not always handle such ideas with
the greatest subtlety or sophistication. When he objected to be-
ing called a pessimist, he would insist that he was an "evolu-
tionary meliorist," whatever that may be; Ransom defines it
with droll finality: "For what is evolutionary meliorism? It is
the synthetic oleomargarine which stern Darwinists used to
spread over the bread of doctrine when they denied themselves
the old-fashioned butter of belief in a moral order." But Hardy
*was* tethered to a philosophy against his will; he said over and
over again that his poems recorded not convictions but im-
pressions. We may well feel that the ideas were necessary to
him; he was by nature a feeler not a reasoner, and without a
carapace of more or less "objective" ideas, he might have been
quite overwhelmed by his powerful sensibility. He may have
thought of Nature in terms of blind matter and will, random
change, the struggle for existence, but he saw it as fully alive,
full of spirits, a visible world whose intimations led continuously

to an invisible one. Ransom again: "Nature for him was an insoluble ambiguity. From the philosopher in him it exacted the not-so-distinguished tribute of hateful indignation. . . . From the poet it usually got faithful perception and love." His ideas may sometimes make us smile, but they are surely a good deal more humane or at least less harmful than many of Eliot's ideas, or Pound's, and much less silly than many of Yeats's. But in the end the ideas don't really matter. John Bayley, whose book *An Essay on Hardy* is full of tender and radiant insights, puts it beautifully. First he takes issue with John Berryman and Donald Davie, and surely many others, who see the end of "The Darkling Thrush" as ironic, and he argues persuasively that "nothing in the poem is aware of the possibility of being organised for purposes of irony; its participants are preoccupied with their own affairs, the poet not least." And then: "One can suspect that the exasperation felt by so many of his readers at his 'philosophy,' and the emphatic ways in which they drew attention to its anomaly, was because his effect on them—his power to move them in particular—did not really seem much connected with it. Such a hiatus irritated the late Victorian mind, accustomed to continuity between attitude, system, and feeling, alike in Tennyson as in George Eliot." No, the ideas that matter in Hardy are the *poetic* ideas, which are another thing entirely, ideas as much emotional as intellectual, as much technical as emotional, and to be found only in the experience of the poems themselves—the honesty of response, the exactness and delicacy of perception, the seeking after and discovery of right feeling, "the closeness of phrase to vision"—the sense we get from great poetry that the moral and the aesthetic are rarely, if ever, separate things.

His much remarked awkwardness was, like the carelessness that Eliot complained of, largely deliberate—he considered it a warrant for sincerity, and for the most part it does work that way. When he uses his strange mix of language—standard and dialect words, poetical words, rare words, scientific terms, coinages, archaisms—a hodgepodge diction unlike anything else in

English poetry, not to mention the occasionally convoluted syntax and other odd quirks of style, he is after something, some truth, some accuracy of representation. Of course he sometimes fails in the attempt—how could he not in the course of almost a thousand poems?—but it is astonishing how often he succeeds. As E. A. Robinson said once, he may stumble a good deal, but he always gets there. Nor is he as eccentric as he is sometimes made out to be. J.I.M. Stewart has observed that the more intensely Hardy is moved by his subject, the less idiosyncratic his accent and the simpler his diction. What demonstrates the truth of the contention that he usually employs an outlandish language for particular effects is the large number of poems in which he writes very soberly, in the plain style, the syntax simple and direct, the words in their natural order. It happens far too often to be accidental.

His versification can also seem strange at first, for he sounds like no one else. I can think of no other poet who has devised so many and such intricate stanza forms and rhyme schemes—in this he much resembles George Herbert—and the variety of sounds is seemingly endless; as Larkin says, ". . . each [poem] has a little tune of its own, and this is something you can say of very few poets." (It was important to Frost too; he wrote, "Few will dare or deign to dispute that the prime object of composing poetry is to keep any two poems from sounding alike," and commented at a reading that his poems "make so many different sounds—I don't write them all the same day. I have to keep them well separated so they'll *have* different sounds.") Hardy is a master of verse and knows exactly what he's doing. Ransom said that no poet understood the function of meter better than Hardy and had the highest praise for the sureness and delicacy of his ear and his fresh way with the meters, which, he said, "this poet loved with a passion and managed with utmost ingenuity." One beautiful example that comes to mind is "The Missed Train," where his characteristic anapest, with either the first or second unaccented syllable strongly stressed, grows suddenly more frequent and audible in the last two stanzas, heavier and slower, so that "if you have the sense to read without jingling, there is emphasis as it falls in the natural phrasing"—

> *Years, yéars as shoaled séas*
> *Truly, strétch now betwéen! Less and léss*
> *Shrink the vísions then vást in me.—Yés,*
> *Then in mé: Now in thése.*

they seem not so much anapests as amphimacers: "Thén in mé: Nów in thése." The movement of these lines brings tears to my eyes.

He has also been censured sometimes for what seems a tendency to force the rhymes, and it is true that in fulfilling his commitment in complicated stanza forms and intricate rhyme schemes he will occasionally reach for a too poetical word or an eccentric one. But more often he is wondrously dexterous in his rhyming, and it is important to remember that he is rarely very far from song, so that what might sound somewhat forced in a sonnet, say, or heroic couplets comes off easily and naturally enough in the conventions of song, as in

> *Her smiles would have shone*
> *With welcomings. . . . But*
> *She is shut, she is shut*
> > *From friendship's spell*
> > *In the jailing shell*
> > *Of her tiny cell.*

or in the even more abruptly enjambed line two stanzas later,

> *And peered in the rime*
> *Of Candlemas-time*
> *For crocuses. . . . chanced*
> *It that she were not tranced*
> > *From sights she loved best;*
> > *Wholly possessed*
> > *By an infinite rest!*

—which doesn't seem all that different from a beautiful run-on rhyme I heard in a Randy Travis song not very long ago:

> *I need your love, I miss it;*
> *We can't go on like this—it*
> *Húrts toó múch!*

Hardy would have relished that, having taken up the measures of his own country singers.

*       *       *       *

Poor Hardy—he also makes trouble for the professors by having been so inconsiderate as to be born too early and die too late, so not fitting comfortably into any of the convenient academic categories. Is he a Victorian or a modern? A Victorian novelist and a modern poet? Or perhaps the other way round, as one rash soul has ventured? Even Mr. Ransom, one of his most loving and discerning critics, worries a little about where to put him. I think that no one has addressed this question with more insight or more humility than Ransom's old fellow Fugitive, Donald Davidson:

> Hardy wrote, or tried to write, more or less as a modern—modern, for him, being late nineteenth century. But he thought, or artistically conceived, like a man of another century—indeed, of a century that we should be hard put to name. It might be better to say that he wrote like a creator of tales and poems who is a little embarrassed at having to adapt the creation of tales and poems to the condition of a written, or printed, literature, and yet tries to do his faithful best under the regrettable circumstances. He is not in any sense a "folk author" and yet he does approach his tale-telling and poem-making as if three centuries of Renaissance effort had worked only upon the out-

ward form of tale and poem without changing its essential character. . . .

Hardy is the only specimen of his genus in modern English literature, and I do not know how to account for him. He has no immediate predecessors. . . .

Hardy made poems continually out of whatever material came to hand or mind. Making them was simply his way of being in the world, and anything he ever saw, heard, felt, thought, read about, was grist for his mill. Over a period of seventy years, more or less, he was bound to write some bad ones—but he took his chances and, more often than not, he scored. For example: on April 15, 1900, Hardy wrote in his notebook, "Easter Sunday. Watched a blackbird on a budding sycamore. Was near enough to see his tongue, and crocus-coloured bill parting and closing as he sang. He flew down, picked up a stem of hay, and flew up to where he was building." With remarkably few changes, mostly to get it moving in meter and to nail the rhymes, this became a poem:

> I *watched a blackbird on a budding sycamore*
> One Easter Day, *when sap was stirring twigs to the core;*
> I *saw his tongue, and crocus-coloured bill*
> *Parting and closing as he turned his trill;*
> *Then he flew down, seized on a stem of hay,*
> *And upped to where his building scheme was under way,*
> *As if so sure a nest were never shaped on spray.*

Next to nothing added to the original rapt observation. Slight, yes, but lovely, and many of us would be pleased to have written it.

Such poems tell us something about the naturalness and purity of the man, alert to the tiniest events, things that go unnoticed by most people, or if noticed, not regarded as very important. Virginia Woolf paid Hardy a visit in 1926; it's not unlikely that the famous dog Wessex tried to bite her, but the old man was very glad to see her, her father, Leslie Stephen, having been a great friend of his for more than thirty years, as well as one of the first editors to help him establish himself as a professional writer. She wrote a charming account of the visit in *A Writer's Diary*:

> Indeed, there was no trace to my thinking of the simple peasant. He seemed perfectly aware of everything; in no doubt or hesitation; having made up his mind; and being delivered of all of his work, so that he was in no doubt about that either. He was not interested much in his novels, or in anybody's novels; took it all easily and naturally. . . . He seemed to be free of it all; very active-minded; liking to describe people, not to talk in an abstract way; for example Col. Lawrence, bicycling with a broken arm "held like that". . . . There was not a trace anywhere of deference to editors, or respect for rank or extreme simplicity. What impressed me was his freedom, ease and vitality. He seemed very "Great Victorian" doing the whole thing with a sweep of his hand (they are ordinary smallish, curled up hands) and setting no great stock by literature, but immensely interested in facts; incidents; and somehow, one could imagine, naturally swept off into imagining and creating without a thought of its being difficult or remarkable; becoming obsessed; and living in imagination. . . .
> [*Speaking of the books of the day, Hardy said*] "They've changed everything now. We used to think there was a beginning and a middle and an end. We believed in the Aristotelian theory. Now one of those stories came to an end with a woman going out of the room." He chuckled. But he no longer reads novels. The whole thing—literature, novels, etc., all seemed to him an amusement, far away too, scarcely to be taken seriously. Yet he had sympathy and pity for

those still engaged in it. But what his secret interests and activities are—to what occupation he trotted off when we left him—I do not know. Small boys write to him from New Zealand and have to be answered. They bring out a "Hardy number" of a Japanese paper, which he produced. Talked too about Blunden. I think Mrs. Hardy keeps him posted in the doings of the younger poets.

He was always open to new things and interested in what was going on, and he was not too proud to learn from lesser poets. (He was not proud at all.) Eliot may have found Hardy's work hard to swallow, but Hardy thought Eliot's poems very interesting. He admired "The Love Song of J. Alfred Prufrock" and copied passages from it into his notebook. And in spite of his dislike of *vers libre* (he wrote to a friend, "the original sinner was Whitman, who, I always think, wrote as he did, formlessly, because he could do no better"), he read "The Waste Land" with great care, made notes and copied parts of it too in his notebook. Although he had but seven or eight years of formal schooling, he became a rather learned man, and he seems to have read every poem he could lay his hands on. He liked Emily Dickinson very much and copied out a couple of her poems, "Apparently with no surprise" and "I died for beauty"—both of them rather Hardyesque, aren't they.

Hardyesque, but not Hardy. Hardy's voice is always immediately recognizable—he is inimitably himself. But he can enter deeply and sympathetically into an astonishing variety of lives. In this selection alone, he assumes the voices of an old maid, a whore, a carpenter, the ghost of his wife, a trampwoman, falling leaves, a widow, a man about to abandon his family, a frightened young bride, a dog, Death, the moon, a star, rooks and starlings, jilted swains, old soldiers, God, and a calf! And this brings me to another quality, perhaps the most beautiful of all, which I have touched on only lightly, the quality that one writer has tried to describe by saying that Hardy's poems are not written for us, or for *any* audience one can think of—we overhear him as he speaks to himself. Many readers have felt him to be the least pretentious of writers. He pays the closest attention to his subject, to the rhyme and meter, everything that goes into the making of a poem, but seemingly without the least consciousness of what anyone may think of it—even himself. Inside this attentive, skillful, practiced artist is someone utterly innocent and undesigning. One never feels in Hardy, as in Yeats, say, any effort to dazzle. He is not interested in dazzle, he is interested in the truth, in the song. In hundreds of poems he looks out at the world with an eyelid's soundless blink—an eye without an I. He has no fear of sentiment or of the obvious; he has none of our hard, modern knowingness. There is a beautiful epigram by Walter Sickert that made me think of Hardy the first time I came across it: "The whole of art is one long roll of revelation, and it is revealed only to those whose minds are to some extent what Horace, speaking of a woman whose heart is free, calls vacant. It is not for those whose minds are muddied with the dirt of politics, or heated with the vulgar chatter of society." Bayley sometimes comes closer than anyone to anatomizing this innocence in Hardy: he says that Hardy seems not "to possess a self in any of the senses to which the romantic poets and theorists, the philosophers and the novelists, have accustomed us. His presence is much more indeterminately personal, self-delighting but not self-scrutinising, a tremulous tender fleeting entity, like the Emperor Hadrian's *'animula vagula blandula'*—a phrase which must have held an appeal for Hardy, for he quotes it more than once." (This phrase, essentially untranslatable, might possibly be rendered as "little charmer, wayward little soul of mine.") He has a kind of purity and inwardness that is uncommon in poets—in people, come to that. He does not perform, he is not looking our way, he has no need to impress us. Here is Bayley again, speaking about the "extraordinary happiness" in "A Procession of Dead Days," as Hardy greets each day, each one quite oblivious of all the others: "The absorption is wonderfully endearing, yet, as a phrase like

—'Ah, this one. Yes, I know his name'—shows, it is the kind
of rapt and homely absorption that would once have belonged
to devotional poetry." And then: ". . . Stinsford was holy
ground to Hardy as his church at Bemerton was to Herbert—
except for the dogma the location rested in. The fervour comes
home to us as if we shared an essential orthodoxy, which in a
sense we do, for Hardy is the reverse of heretical. He does not
substitute a new belief or attitude but continues in the old one,
having ceased to believe it. His poetry is an aspect of the liturgy,
God having as solid an existence in his art as he did in the old
worship. For the saints, and a saintly poet like Herbert, humour
is part of a secure belief, and it is typical that Hardy still assumes
this kind of security, the belief having gone." I find this insight
brilliant and true and moving. And perhaps it is for this quality
that we love Hardy and overlook, or even enjoy, the bad po-
ems, bad poems such as only a great poet could have written.
John Crowe Ransom speaks for all of us who

> consent to the charge that Hardy is an uneven poet,
> and capable of marring fine poems by awkward and
> tasteless passages; and even of writing whole poems
> that now are too harsh, and again are too merely pe-
> destrian. For some reason, however, I must confess
> that these lapses have often seemed to endear the poet
> to me. . . . and I can think of but one way to ra-
> tionalize so odd a reception: by the consideration that
> "bad form," though generally a thing to be repre-
> hended, is possibly under one circumstance to be ap-
> proved: where we feel that the ignorance behind it
> is the condition of the innocence and spontaneity we
> admire.

*   *   *   *

"I can say no more; I have even said too much." James Gibson,
in a recent letter, seems to have summed up my essay in a single
sentence: "The range of subject-matter, the assumption that

poetry can be about anything and should be available to everybody, the tenderness, the wisdom, the honesty, the loving-kindness beneath so much of what he wrote, the incredible technical skill and the erudition. . . . they never cease to astonish me." I shall leave the last word to Ezra Pound: "A conscientious critic might be hard put to it to find just praise for Hardy's poems. When a writer's matter is stated with such entirety and such clarity there is no place left for the explaining critic. . . . Poem after poem of Hardy's leaves one with nowt more to say."

# CHRONOLOGY

1821        Napoleon Bonaparte dies in exile on St. Helena.

1840        Thomas Hardy is born on June 2 in Higher Bock-hampton, a hamlet near Dorchester, about five months after his parents' wedding. His father, Thomas, although easygoing and not especially ambitious, is a modestly successful stonemason (as *his* father, also named Thomas, was) and a builder, employing several men. His mother, Jemima (whose drunken, violent father died when she was a child, leaving the family penniless and dependent on parish charity), has ambition enough for both of them, and she is determined that her own children will be educated and will never have to do the menial work that *she* has done all her life.

1841        His sister Mary is born.

1844        He is given an accordion by his father, and begins to learn to play the fiddle.

1847        The railroad reaches Dorchester.

1848        Hardy attends the village school. He has already been reading for several years, and his mother, who is herself a passionate reader, is giving her son such books as Dryden's *Virgil* and Johnson's *Rasselas*. (His godfather has given him *The Rites and Worship of the Jews*.)

1850    He is enrolled in Isaac Last's Dorchester British School because his mother believes he will get a better education there than in the village school; she pays a supplemental fee for his instruction in Latin. (Pound wrote in 1964 that "no man ever had so much Latin and so eschewed the least appearance of being a classicist on the surface.") He is now walking six miles every day, back and forth between a "world of ploughmen and shepherds"—a folk culture largely unchanged since the Middle Ages—and "a county-town . . . which had advanced to railways and telegraphs and daily London papers."

1851    His brother Henry is born.

1855    He begins to teach in the Stinsford Parish Sunday School.

1856    End of formal education. He is apprenticed to John Hicks, a Dorchester architect, and becomes friends with William Barnes (then almost sixty), who keeps a school next door to Hicks's office. Barnes is a learned philologist and a divine, and a good poet, who has sacrificed any chance for lasting fame by his insistence on writing in the Dorset dialect. Hardy's sister Katherine is born.

1857    His paternal grandmother dies. He is rising well before dawn every day and studying for three or four hours before setting off for Dorchester, improving his Latin and teaching himself Greek, with occasional help from his friend Horace Moule, who has taken courses at Oxford and at Cambridge.

1858    Hardy is beginning to write poetry. "Domicilium," his earliest surviving poem, dates from this period.

1862        He moves to London to work for the noted architect
            Arthur Blomfield and to study architecture and
            church restoration. He explores the city, goes to
            plays and to the opera as often as possible, attends a
            Dickens lecture, has his head examined by a phre-
            nologist, and spends a great deal of time in the Na-
            tional Gallery and the British Museum. Reading
            Fourier, Huxley, Darwin, Comte, and Mill, he is
            beginning to question the tenets of his faith and at-
            tends church a little less religiously, but a country
            curacy is still one of his dreams of a possible future,
            as well as literary journalism, art criticism, and
            architecture.

1865–66     He begins studying French in an evening class, and
            he is reading Shakespeare, Spenser, Gray, Thomson,
            Wordsworth, and Tennyson—like many young
            men he is very excited by Swinburne's first book.
            He is writing a good deal of verse. He sends out a
            few poems to the magazines but they are quickly
            rejected and he destroys some of them—to his later
            regret.

1867        He thinks of becoming an actor and takes part in a
            pantomime at Covent Garden; that is the end of his
            theatrical career. His health worn down by city life,
            the bad air, and late hours, he gladly accepts an in-
            vitation from Hicks to come back to Dorchester and
            work in his office again. There he begins his first
            novel, *The Poor Man and the Lady*, which attacks en-
            trenched privilege and the class system, a book that
            would be rejected the following year and soon af-
            terward destroyed.

1869        He moves to Weymouth to work for another ar-
            chitect, G. R. Crickmay. He rows and swims in the

1869    ocean every day and attends a dancing class, "the so-called class," he wrote later, "being, in fact, a gay gathering for dances and love-making by adepts of both sexes."

1870    He journeys to Cornwall on Crickmay's request to make measurements and drawings for the restoration of a church in St. Juliot, and there meets Emma Lavinia Gifford, the rector's sister-in-law. She is a handsome, lively young woman of Hardy's age (though she claims to be twenty-five). She is not impressed by Hardy at first—he is shorter than she, and slight—but she is badly in need of a serious suitor, and Hardy is clearly attracted to her. As Larkin puts it, "Certainly for a middle-class woman of thirty in North Cornwall in 1870 sixteen miles from the nearest railway station to get a husband, some kind of divine intervention seems imperative"—or at least a conspiracy, and with help from her sister, with whom she does not get on very well, she sets out to capture him. She is literary, provocative, full of vitality, and has a kind of fey charm. She rides her horse over the hills in all weathers, and she seems to Hardy to be a free spirit. They go on walks and picnics along the banks of the Valency and the cliffs overlooking the Atlantic surf. When Hardy leaves, it is understood that he will be back, and indeed he does return in August to continue his courtship. Very likely Emma has permitted him certain sexual intimacies. (If one of his poems can be taken as having some autobiographical truth, she may, like Arabella in *Jude the Obscure*, have pretended that she was pregnant.)

1871    Although his first book is turned down by Macmillan, the publisher and one of his readers, who, as it happens, is the well-known novelist George Meredith, encourage Hardy to go on writing. He publishes his second novel, *Desperate Remedies*, at his own expense, and finishes another, *Under the Greenwood Tree*. More visits to beautiful Cornwall.

1872–73   *Under the Greewood Tree* is published; the reviews are generally good. He lives in London for a while, working for an architect, and meets Leslie Stephen, who will be a very good friend, and a great influence. Stephen invites him to submit a novel for serialization in the *Cornhill Magazine*, which he edits —this is a great stroke of fortune; it will launch the young writer's career. In the summer of 1872, with Emma's support, indeed with her strong encouragement, Hardy takes perhaps the most decisive step of his life: he abandons architecture and ventures everything on a literary career. *A Pair of Blue Eyes* is published the following year. Hardy's closest friend, Horace Moule, commits suicide in his rooms at Cambridge. There are more visits to Cornwall, then a disastrous one to Bodmin to see Emma's snobbish and hostile father. Although Hardy has misgivings, he and Emma are planning to marry.

1874   Hardy marries Emma Lavinia Gifford on September 17 in a nondescript London church, with only two guests (the obligatory witnesses), Emma's brother, and Hardy's landlady's daughter—not an auspicious beginning. They honeymoon in France, and on their return, rent a house in Surbiton, a London suburb. *Far from the Madding Crowd*, which was a popular serial, is published in two volumes. It is his first great novel: almost all the reviews are laudatory and enthusiastic, the first edition quickly sells out, and Hardy is famous.

1875–78    Summoned by Stephen, Hardy witnesses his mentor's formal renunciation of holy orders. He and Emma travel in Holland and Germany. *The Hand of Ethelberta* is published. After several moves, they take a house in Sturminster Newton; their two years there Hardy will later recall as the happiest period of their marriage. Another major novel, *The Return of the Native*, is published.

1879–82    After a stay in London, they return to Dorset and live in various places, including Weymouth. There are already strains in their relationship. Their hopes for a child have been disappointed; Emma is jealous of Hardy's growing fame and compensates by reminding herself that she has married beneath her; Jemima has never been warm to Emma, who in her eyes has neither youth nor wealth nor domestic skills to recommend her, and she scorns Emma's pretensions to gentility; Hardy talks to his family about his desire to build a house nearby and they all concur; Emma, who dreams of living in London and dining with the rich and famous, has no say in the matter and she is understandably angry about her exclusion—she will never really be accepted by this close, even clannish, family, and she will retaliate. In 1880 Hardy survives a long and serious illness, which seems to have begun with a bladder infection and an internal hemorrhage. During these years, he meets Tennyson, Browning, Arnold, and James. Although he dislikes James personally and jokes about his "ponderously warm manner of saying nothing in infinite sentences," he admires his work and sometimes says that he is the only contemporary novelist he can read. (James in turn does not much care for Hardy's work—he has written a rather condescending review of *Far from the Madding Crowd*—and he refers to him as "good little Thomas Hardy.") Hardy's publisher is now Macmillan; between 1880 and 1882, several minor novels appear. In April of 1882, he attends Darwin's funeral in Westminster Abbey.

1883    He and Emma move back to Dorchester. His father and brother and their men begin the building of Max Gate. Hardy, who designed the villa down to the last detail, supervises the construction, not without strain and the occasional argument. He is by now a distinguished man of letters and earning a great deal of money; he and Emma begin their habit of going to London every spring or summer and staying for "the season," usually two or three months.

1885    They move into the large and comfortable redbrick house at Max Gate. Emma cannot have been very happy: she was now permanently in Jemima's territory, and for most of the year deprived of the glittering social life that she had fantasized would be hers as the wife of a famous writer. The sad reality of being a writer's wife was that she was largely left to her own devices. As Michael Millgate, Hardy's best biographer, puts it, "The study was always for Hardy the heart of the house. Though its location shifted, it was always upstairs, as far as possible removed from household activities and callers at the front door, and always impregnable, except by rare invitation to especially favored visitors. It was there that Hardy, to the very end of his life, spent the greater part of almost every day."

1886–88  William Barnes dies and Hardy writes an obituary for the *Atheneum*. (Although he felt great affection for the old man, and gratitude, there had also been a suppressed sense of rivalry, and now Wessex was

1886–88    all his—as Kipling joked in "The Rhyme of the
Three Captains," he was "Lord of the Wessex coast
and all the lands thereby.") He meets Walter Pater,
"whose manner," he writes, "is that of one carrying
weighty ideas without spilling them." *The Mayor of
Casterbridge* and *The Woodlanders* are published, ar-
guably his two greatest novels and each a critical and
popular success. Hardy is especially gratified by
Robert Louis Stevenson's regard for them. He and
Emma travel to Italy; in Rome, they visit the graves
of Shelley and Keats. *Wessex Tales* is published.

1889       Hardy is hard at work on his new book, *Tess of the
D'Urbervilles*. The editors at Tillotson (a syndicated
fiction business, distributing serials to newspapers
and magazines) have contracted for the work, but
they are greatly distressed by its frank sexuality and
its author's unconcealed admiration for his heroine,
and ask for some changes, which Hardy refuses to
make. The contract is canceled by mutual consent.
Two magazines turn *Tess* down, and finally Hardy
cuts out the seduction scene, with "cynical amuse-
ment," as he says, and revises and bowdlerizes the
rest until it is acceptable to yet another magazine,
knowing that he will be able to restore it to its orig-
inal shape when it is published in book form.

1890       On a brief trip to London, he meets the young Rud-
yard Kipling, whose stories and poems he greatly
admires. *The Graphic*, the magazine that finally ac-
cepts *Tess*, demands still more changes. Hardy fin-
ishes the book to their satisfaction, but he is furious
about the trouble he has been made to go to. And
now there is more serious trouble in his relations
with Emma, which have grown steadily worse. He
had thought her an agnostic in the happy days of

1870, but she is clearly suffering from a religious mania, which sometimes takes the form of extreme fear and hatred of Roman Catholicism. She is appalled by her husband's opinions—or what she thinks they are, the public caricature rather than his actual thought. She solaces herself with her consciousness of her social superiority, but she is stung by her mother-in-law's contempt for "poor gentry"; as she sees things, her husband has his work and his fame, and she has nothing. She has literary aspirations of her own but no talent. She sometimes scolds Hardy in public, which he bears with silent patience—people think him henpecked. Although she would love to live in London and mingle with the high-born and famous, she does not know how to dress or behave and she is regarded by their London friends as silly and affected. Some of the visitors to Max Gate like her, but most find her vain and frivolous. Her husband will be attracted to a series of beautiful and cultivated society women, and although it is highly unlikely that any of these friendships ever took a sexual turn, she is naturally jealous and angry. They have a modus vivendi at Max Gate; they discuss household affairs, they sometimes travel together, but they live and will go on living in more or less permanent estrangement.

1891    *Tess* is finally published in volume form, and although Hardy is as usual preoccupied by a few cruel reviews and some public attacks on his irreligion and immorality, it is greeted with general acclaim and is enormously popular with the public. And now that the new American copyright bill has been signed into law, it will make him rich. But he has always been hypersensitive to criticism, and he suffers more from the attacks than he enjoys his success; he writes

1891          in his notebook, "Well, if this sort of thing contin-
              ues, no more novel-writing for me. A man must be
              a fool to deliberately stand up to be shot at." Assured
              of financial security, he thinks more and more of
              retiring as a novelist and taking up his true art. He
              shaves off his beard, perhaps in preparation.

1892          He is at work on *Jude the Obscure*. In July, his father dies.
              It is a heavy blow, not only to Hardy but to the rela-
              tions between his wife and his mother and sisters. (His
              second wife, Florence, asserted that Emma did not
              from this time on allow them in Max Gate.) Millgate
              writes of the elder Hardy's death, "Once he was gone
              there was no effective buffer between an always im-
              placable Jemima and an Emma who was, in middle
              age, revealing her own capacity for wilful obstinacy."

1893          Hardy meets Florence Henniker in Dublin. She is
              the daughter of Lord Houghton, whom Hardy had
              known; she is beautiful, poised, well educated, a
              novelist herself—in short, everything that Emma is
              not, and Hardy falls in love with her. But she is
              married and devoted to her husband, and Hardy's
              hopes, whatever they may be, are disappointed. He
              continues to pursue her, but without success; it is
              possible that she does not realize the intensity of his
              feelings for her. Nevertheless they remain friends.
              She is the subject of a few passionate poems.

1895–96       *Jude the Obscure*, his last novel, is published, and the
              hostility and savagery it provokes far exceed anything
              Hardy has ever had to endure. One newspaper en-
              titles its review "Jude the Obscene" and an article
              in another refers to him as "Hardy the Degenerate."
              There are positive reviews too, but nothing can
              make up for the anguish caused by the vicious ones.

Even his good friend Edmund Gosse writes a critical review, asking, "What has Providence done to Mr. Hardy that he should rise up in the arable land of Wessex and shake his fist at his Creator?" Emma was predictably outraged by the novel, which she took as a commentary on their marriage; she even seems to have made an attempt to prevent its publication. Hardy's misery during these years will be reflected in a number of poems, notably "Wessex Heights" and "In Tenebris I"—the utterances of "One who, past doubtings all, / Waits in unhope."

1898     Hardy publishes *Wessex Poems*, his first book of verse. Many reviewers think it presumptuous of him to set up as a poet and helpfully advise him to go back to fiction.

1901     *Poems of the Past and Present* is better received than his first book—perhaps the critics are beginning to get used to the idea that Hardy is a poet.

1904     Part I of *The Dynasts* appears, the vast epic drama of the Napoleonic wars, which he has been planning for years and for which he has done an immense amount of research. Hardy's mother dies.

1905     Hardy receives an honorary doctorate of laws from the University of Aberdeen.

1906     The editors at Macmillan are very gloomy about having to publish the second installment of *The Dynasts*, Part I having sold very badly, but they feel that they owe it to one of their most profitable and important authors. An opera by Baron Frederic d'Erlanger, based on *Tess*, has its premiere in Naples; the performance is interrupted by the eruption of Mt. Vesuvius. (The Doomsters strike again.)

1907    Hardy meets Florence Emily Dugdale, who will be-
        come his secretary and research assistant and, even-
        tually, his second wife.

1908    *The Dynasts,* Part III, is published. Hardy edits a vol-
        ume of William Barnes's selected poems.

1909    Hardy declines an invitation to visit the United
        States. He is made governor of Dorchester Grammar
        School. *Time's Laughingstocks* is published.

1910    He is awarded the Order of Merit by Edward VII.

1912    In June, William Butler Yeats and Henry Newbolt
        come down to Max Gate to present Hardy with a gold
        medal from the Royal Society of Literature. (In what
        seems an unusual and inexplicable act of cruelty by
        someone who has been called "the kindliest of men,"
        Hardy will not permit Emma to stay in the room dur-
        ing the presentation—perhaps he is retaliating for her
        persistent public insinuations that she has written some
        of his work.) Emma, who has already had privately
        printed a little book of her ludicrous poems, writes a
        religious tract, some of which seems quite mad, and in-
        deed her odd behavior strikes some visitors as clear ev-
        idence of derangement. Suddenly, on the morning of
        November 27, she dies. Hardy's poems over the next
        few years say almost everything that need be said.

1913    Hardy journeys to St. Juliot—thirty-nine years al-
        most to the day since he first saw Emma at the door
        of the rectory. It is a deeply painful experience and
        he wishes he had not gone, but it produces some of
        the most beautiful of the poems he has been writing
        in the aftermath of Emma's death. He is made an
        honorary doctor of letters by Cambridge University.

1914    Hardy marries Florence Emily Dugdale; he is seventy-eight, she is thirty-five. *Satires of Circumstance*, which includes the great series of elegies, is published. He is horrified by the outbreak of war and reports of atrocities, but for all his mistrust of British imperialism, he believes that his country has no choice but to declare war on Germany. He signs an appeal on behalf of the Belgian refugees, and joins a large group of writers, Galsworthy, Wells, and Chesterton among them, who have agreed to contribute in whatever ways they can to the national interest.

1915    Hardy's beloved sister Mary dies.

1917    *Moments of Vision*, at 160 poems his longest (and, for me, his greatest) book of poems, is published. Hardy spends more and more time in his study; Florence is, not surprisingly, very depressed. He visits a German P.O.W. camp near Dorchester.

1919    The first *Collected Poems* is published, and it will be reprinted again and again. Young poets and writers are beginning to visit Hardy, and in the years following, many will come, including Siegfried Sassoon, Robert Graves, Charlotte Mew, and T. E. Lawrence (lately of Arabia, now an enlisted man stationed at a nearby air base under the name of Shaw); older writers like E. M. Forster and George Bernard Shaw will also come to call. Hardy is particularly fond of Sassoon and Lawrence.

1920    Hardy finally has an indoor bathroom and a water heater installed in Max Gate. He is made an honorary doctor of letters by Oxford. There is a great deal of publicity surrounding his eightieth birthday;

1920          everyone acknowledges him as the grand old man of English letters. Although he had in the last few years begun to realize that he "was no mean power in the contemporary world of poetry," he does not seem to be fully aware of the reverence in which he is generally held.

1921          Hardy watches the filming of *The Mayor of Casterbridge* on location in and around Dorchester. (It is directed by Sidney Morgan; Fred Groves plays Henchard.) He says to his friend Vere H. Collins, ". . . perhaps the cinematograph will take the place of fiction, and novels will die out, leaving only poetry." (This is not the first film made from a Hardy novel: one based on *Tess* was shot in 1913 and *Far from the Madding Crowd* in 1915.)

1922          *Late Lyrics and Earlier* is published; so too are Yeats's *Later Poems*, Eliot's *The Waste Land*, and Joyce's *Ulysses*.

1923          A telephone is installed. Hardy's one play, *The Famous Tragedy of the Queen of Cornwall*, is published. Florence Henniker dies. The Prince of Wales, Victoria's great-grandson, honors the poet by coming to Max Gate for luncheon, during which he says to Hardy, "My mother tells me you have written a book called *Tess of the D'Urbervilles*. I must try to read it some time."

1925          *Human Shows* is published. The first printing of 5,000 copies is sold out in a day; whatever hesitation or disapproval may be felt by the professional critics, clearly Hardy is loved by many thousands of common readers.

1926        Virginia Woolf visits Hardy. He talks about his long
            friendship with her father; he remembers seeing
            her in her cradle. Wessex, the notorious and bad-
            tempered dog who has tried to attack almost every
            guest at Max Gate except T. E. Lawrence, dies.
            Hardy visits, for the last time, the cottage in Bock-
            hampton and the Stinsford graveyard, to him "the
            most hallowed place on earth."

1927        Hardy is preparing *Winter Words*, which he imagines
            will be his last book. On December 11, he finds
            himself for the first time unable to work.

1928        Hardy dies on January 11. Although he has always
            wanted to lie in Stinsford beside the graves of Emma
            and Mary and his parents, and has made his wishes
            clear in his will, his friend James Barrie and Sydney
            Cockerell, his literary executor, manage to over-
            come the resistance of his distraught widow and use
            their influence to obtain permission for his burial in
            Westminster Abbey—an honor denied to other re-
            nowned unbelievers such as Swinburne and Mere-
            dith. In a grotesque compromise, his heart is cut out,
            to be buried in the Stinsford churchyard. (A story,
            almost certainly apocryphal but very Hardyesque,
            will allege that the household cat had leapt onto the
            table, seized the heart in its jaws, and run off with
            it into the nearby woods.) There is a simultaneous
            funeral for the ashes of the rest of him in Westmin-
            ster Abbey, where the pallbearers include Barrie,
            A. E. Housman, Sir Edmund Gosse, Rudyard Kip-
            ling, George Bernard Shaw, John Galsworthy, and
            the prime minister, Stanley Baldwin. A good many
            other great literary figures of the day are in atten-
            dance. *Winter Words* is published; so is *The Earlier
            Life of Thomas Hardy*, which appears under the name

1928        of Florence Emily Hardy but was in fact written and
            dictated by Hardy himself during the last few years.
            (*The Later Years of Thomas Hardy*, also his own work
            for the most part, will appear in 1930.)

1929        Hitler consolidates control of the National Socialist
            Party; in four years, he will be chancellor of the
            Third Reich.

# SUGGESTIONS FOR FURTHER READING

Auden, W. H. "A Literary Transference." *Southern Review*, Summer 1940.

Bailey, J. O. *The Poetry of Thomas Hardy: A Handbook and Commentary*. Chapel Hill: University of North Carolina Press, 1970.

Baker, Howard. "Hardy's Poetic Certitude." *Southern Review*, Summer 1940.

Bayley, John. *An Essay on Hardy*. Cambridge: Cambridge University Press, 1978.

Gibson, James, ed. *The Complete Poems of Thomas Hardy*. New York: Macmillan, 1978.

Guerard, Albert, ed. *Thomas Hardy: A Collection of Critical Essays*. Englewood Cliffs, NJ: Prentice-Hall, 1963.

Gunn, Thom. "Hardy and the Ballads," *The Occasions of Poetry*. San Francisco: North Point Press, 1985.

Hardy, Florence Emily. *The Life of Thomas Hardy, 1840–1928*. London: Macmillan, 1962.

Hynes, Samuel, ed. *The Complete Poetical Works of Thomas Hardy*. Oxford: Oxford University Press, Vol. 1, 1982; Vol. 2, 1984; Vol. 3, 1985.

Larkin, Philip. "Wanted: Good Hardy Critic" and "The Poetry of Hardy." *Required Writing*. New York: Farrar, Straus & Giroux, 1982.

Millgate, Michael. *Thomas Hardy: A Biography*. New York: Random House, 1982.

———, ed. *Selected Letters of Thomas Hardy*. Oxford: Oxford University Press, 1990.

Ransom, John Crowe. "Honey and Gall." *Southern Review*, Summer 1940.

————. Introduction to *Selected Poems of Thomas Hardy*. New York: Macmillan, 1961.

Schwartz, Delmore. "Poetry and Belief in Thomas Hardy." *Southern Review*, Summer 1940.

Taylor, Dennis. *Hardy's Metres and Victorian Prosody*. Oxford: Oxford University Press, 1988.

————. *Hardy's Poetry, 1860–1928*. London: Macmillan, 1989.

Zabel, Morton Dauwen. "Hardy in Defense of His Art: The Aesthetic of Incongruity." *Southern Review*, Summer 1940.

# NOTE ON THE SELECTION

More than one editor has felt the need to join in the ritual apology that Hardy resists selection, that there is little agreement about which poems best display his greatness and his characteristic qualities, and that one's own selection must needs be personal and subjective. It is easy to understand what prompts these concessions. Anyone who has already fallen under his spell will want all 950 or so poems to wander around in. As Philip Larkin has said, "One can read him for years and years and still be surprised, and I think that's a marvellous thing to find in any poet."

Larkin also "trumpet[s] the assurance that one reader at least would not wish Hardy's *Collected Poems* a single page shorter. . . ." There is a touch of truculent exaggeration in that assurance, considering Larkin's fastidiousness in publishing his own very slender books, but I know what he means. There is much to be said for reading Hardy's poems by the hundreds, and I would readily agree that no selection can take the place of the vast jungle of *The Complete Poems*, where one may come across a poem one has not seen for years and forgotten, or nearly forgotten, and find it lovely, in part or all, and realize too that in certain respects the lesser poems are often not dramatically different from the greater poems. But even granting all this, I do not assent to the commonplace claim that every selection can be no more than merely personal—a claim belied by the fact that every editor has done a considerable amount of work and gone to some trouble to present his selected Hardy to the public: surely he must believe that his "merely personal" selection is the best. In any case, I am addressing myself here to those readers of poetry who have not yet read Hardy, or who know him only by the four or five standards that are continually recycled in the anthologies. (There, there is all too *much* agreement.) Those who already love him and know him will take their satisfaction in finding this selection, like all the others, unsatisfactory.

Hardy, when he was editing a selection of William Barnes's poems, took note of just those perplexities that confront an editor selecting *his* poems. He wrote that "many a poem of indifferent achievement in its wholeness may contain some line, couplet, or stanza of great excellence; and contrariwise, a bad or irrelevant verse may mar the good remainder; in each case the choice is puzzled, and the balance struck by a single mind can hardly escape being questioned here and there." Choosing a hundred of Hardy's finest poems was easy; it was the next seventy or eighty that were rather hard to settle on. There are hundreds of poems that I am fond of or find interesting, but given my limitations of space, I wanted a modest number of fully realized poems that would attract readers who do not already know that Hardy is one of the greatest poets in our language. I have also kept in mind a useful remark by Ezra Pound: "In the midst of a mass (800 pages good and bad together) of quite ordinary verse and verse experiment, one wants to make a valid selection, implying the history of Hardy's technical biography, a technique consisting largely in sloughing off all that wasn't the essential Hardy and only Hardy. . . ." My selection makes it clear that, for me, the essential Hardy is a master of the plain style, the maker of such poems as "The House of Hospitalities," "After the Last Breath," "My Spirit Will Not Haunt the Mound," "At Castle Boterel," "Old Furniture," "No Buyers," "One Who Married Above Him," and so many more, all unmistakably Hardy but for the most part free of his more striking idiosyncrasies. Although a number of his finest poems are admittedly eccentric in style, he is generally at his best when his diction is most direct and simple. I believe that my other criteria are implicit in my remarks on individual poems, either in my notes or in the introductory essay.

I know that I have omitted a few poems that perhaps some

readers will miss—"The Subalterns," for example—but I have not kept any poem that I do not wholeheartedly like. I have also been forced by economic considerations to omit some poems that I would otherwise certainly have included. Although Hardy died childless seventy years ago and is by now part of our common patrimony, his last two books are still "owned" by a large publishing house which aims to make as much money as possible out of them in the last year or so before they join the earlier books in the public domain. I have therefore dropped five or ten poems that I love or admire, among them "The Later Autumn," "On the Esplanade," and "Silences."

For all my confidence in my own judgment, I have tested a great many of my choices against the opinions of a few friends, poets themselves, for whose literary taste and intelligence I have immense respect, and while I did not always accept their advice, I took it under advisement and relied on it more often than not in making up my mind about poems I was not sure of. They suggested a few beautiful pieces I had overlooked, and they induced me to drop most of the few poems for which my affection is "merely personal." Needless to say, they are not responsible for any of my errors or misjudgments. They have my warmest thanks—David Ferry, Peter Everwine, John Hollander, Ronald Goodman, Edgar Bowers, Dick Barnes, and most of all, Donald Justice, who was as always very generous with his time; his close and attentive reading of my manuscript supplied me with scores of useful suggestions. I am grateful to Thomas Pinney for his great learning and his knowledge of Hardy, not to mention his always sharp eye for my solecisms and infelicities; I am a better writer for his help. I wish to express thanks to Laurie Glover, who did almost all of the collating and ascertaining of the texts with her customary care and patience; and to Esther Cristol, who was kind enough to send me some material that I had not seen and that proved very useful. I am deeply indebted to many scholars and critics, especially Dennis Taylor, Donald Davidson, John Bayley, and my dear teacher, John Crowe Ransom. It should go without saying that no scholar or editor can write about Hardy without gratitude for the loving labor and intelligence of James Gibson and of Samuel Hynes, both for their writings about Hardy's poetry and for their exemplary editions, Gibson for *The Complete Poems of Thomas Hardy*, Macmillan, 1976, and Hynes for *The Complete Poetical Works of Thomas Hardy*, Oxford University Press, 1982–85. The books of J. O. Bailey, F. B. Pinion, and Alan Hurst have been helpful to me, as they have no doubt been helpful to a great many readers, and I cannot imagine what I would do without Michael Millgate's scrupulous and admirable biography, *Thomas Hardy*. I owe particular thanks to Dr. Gibson and his wife Helen for their several kindnesses and generosities to me and to Donald and Jean Justice when we sojourned in Dorset; and also to Mr. and Mrs. Andrew Leah, the present tenants of Max Gate, for their friendly welcome and for a poignant perambulation of the house and grounds. And not least, my heartfelt thanks to Eileen for her love and encouragement, and her long endurance of my quirks and obsessions.

# SELECTED POEMS

# DOMICILIUM

It faces west, and round the back and sides
High beeches, bending, hang a veil of boughs,
And sweep against the roof. Wild honeysucks
Climb on the walls, and seem to sprout a wish
(If we may fancy wish of trees and plants)
To overtop the apple-trees hard by.

Red roses, lilacs, variegated box
Are there in plenty, and such hardy flowers
As flourish best untrained. Adjoining these
Are herbs and esculents; and farther still
A field; then cottages with trees, and last
The distant hills and sky.

Behind, the scene is wilder. Heath and furze
Are everything that seems to grow and thrive
Upon the uneven ground. A stunted thorn
Stands here and there, indeed; and from a pit
An oak uprises, springing from a seed
Dropped by some bird a hundred years ago.

                              In days bygone—
Long gone—my father's mother, who is now
Blest with the blest, would take me out to walk.
At such a time I once inquired of her
How looked the spot when first she settled here.
The answer I remember. "Fifty years
Have passed since then, my child, and change has marked
The face of all things. Yonder garden-plots
And orchards were uncultivated slopes
O'ergrown with bramble bushes, furze and thorn:
That road a narrow path shut in by ferns,

30 Which, almost trees, obscured the passer-by.
   "Our house stood quite alone, and those tall firs
   And beeches were not planted. Snakes and efts
   Swarmed in the summer days, and nightly bats
   Would fly about our bedrooms. Heathcroppers
35 Lived on the hills, and were our only friends;
   So wild it was when first we settled here."

From
WESSEX POEMS
AND
OTHER VERSES

# HAP

If but some vengeful god would call to me
From up the sky, and laugh: "Thou suffering thing,
Know that thy sorrow is my ecstasy,
That thy love's loss is my hate's profiting!"

5  Then would I bear it, clench myself, and die,
Steeled by the sense of ire unmerited;
Half-eased in that a Powerfuller than I
Had willed and meted me the tears I shed.

But not so. How arrives it joy lies slain,
10  And why unblooms the best hope ever sown?
—Crass Casualty obstructs the sun and rain,
And dicing Time for gladness casts a moan. . . .
These purblind Doomsters had as readily strown
Blisses about my pilgrimage as pain.

*1866*

# NEUTRAL TONES

We stood by a pond that winter day,
And the sun was white, as though chidden of God,
And a few leaves lay on the starving sod;
        —They had fallen from an ash, and were gray.

5  Your eyes on me were as eyes that rove
Over tedious riddles of years ago;
And some words played between us to and fro
        On which lost the more by our love.

The smile on your mouth was the deadest thing
10  Alive enough to have strength to die;
And a grin of bitterness swept thereby
    Like an ominous bird a-wing. . . .

Since then, keen lessons that love deceives,
And wrings with wrong, have shaped to me
15  Your face, and the God-curst sun, and a tree,
    And a pond edged with grayish leaves.

                                        *1867*


## SHE, TO HIM II

Perhaps, long hence, when I have passed away,
Some other's feature, accent, thought like mine,
Will carry you back to what I used to say,
And bring some memory of your love's decline.

5  Then you may pause awhile and think, "Poor jade!"
And yield a sigh to me—as ample due,
Not as the tittle of a debt unpaid
To one who could resign her all to you—

And thus reflecting, you will never see
10  That your thin thought, in two small words conveyed,
Was no such fleeting phantom-thought to me,
But the Whole Life wherein my part was played;
And you amid its fitful masquerade
A Thought—as I in your life seem to be!

                                        *1866*

# Friends Beyond

William Dewy, Tranter Reuben, Farmer Ledlow late at
plough,
    Robert's kin, and John's, and Ned's,
And the Squire, and Lady Susan, lie in Mellstock churchyard
now!

"Gone," I call them, gone for good, that group of local
hearts and heads;
    Yet at mothy curfew-tide,
And at midnight when the noon-heat breathes it back from
walls and leads,

They've a way of whispering to me—fellow-wight who yet
abide—
    In the muted, measured note
Of a ripple under archways, or a lone cave's stillicide:

"We have triumphed: this achievement turns the bane to
antidote,
    Unsuccesses to success,
Many thought-worn eves and morrows to a morrow free of
thought.

"No more need we corn and clothing, feel of old terrestrial
stress;
    Chill detraction stirs no sigh;
Fear of death has even bygone us: death gave all that we
possess."

*W.D.*—"Ye mid burn the old bass-viol that I set such value
by."

*Squire.*—"You may hold the manse in fee,
   You may wed my spouse, may let my children's memory
         of me die."

*Lady S.*—"You may have my rich brocades, my laces; take
         each household key;
20       Ransack coffer, desk, bureau;
   Quiz the few poor treasures hid there, con the letters kept
         by me."

*Far.*—"Ye mid zell my favourite heifer, ye mid let the char-
         lock grow,
   Foul the grinterns, give up thrift."
*Far. Wife.*—"If ye break my best blue china, children, I
         shan't care or ho."

25 *All.*—"We've no wish to hear the tidings, how the people's
         fortunes shift;
   What your daily doings are;
   Who are wedded, born, divided; if your lives beat slow
         or swift.

   "Curious not the least are we if our intents you make or
         mar,
   If you quire to our old tune,
30 If the City stage still passes, if the weirs still roar afar."

   —Thus, with very gods' composure, freed those crosses late
         and soon
   Which, in life, the Trine allow
   (Why, none witteth), and ignoring all that haps beneath the
         moon,

   William Dewy, Tranter Reuben, Farmer Ledlow late at
         plough,
35    Robert's kin, and John's, and Ned's,
   And the Squire, and Lady Susan, murmur mildly to me now.

## NATURE'S QUESTIONING

When I look forth at dawning, pool,
    Field, flock, and lonely tree,
    All seem to gaze at me
Like chastened children sitting silent in a school;

Their faces dulled, constrained, and worn,
    As though the master's way
    Through the long teaching day
Had cowed them till their early zest was overborne.

Upon them stirs in lippings mere
    (As if once clear in call,
    But now scarce breathed at all)—
"We wonder, ever wonder, why we find us here!

"Has some Vast Imbecility,
    Mighty to build and blend,
    But impotent to tend,
Framed us in jest, and left us now to hazardry?

"Or come we of an Automaton
    Unconscious of our pains? . . .
    Or are we live remains
Of Godhead dying downwards, brain and eye now gone?

"Or is it that some high Plan betides,
    As yet not understood,
    Of Evil stormed by Good,
We the Forlorn Hope over which Achievement strides?"

25      Thus things around. No answerer I. . . .
         Meanwhile the winds, and rains,
         And·Earth's old glooms and pains
Are still the same, and Life and Death are neighbours nigh.


## In a Eweleaze near Weatherbury

The years have gathered grayly
    Since I danced upon this leaze
With one who kindled gaily
    Love's fitful ecstasies!
5   But despite the term as teacher,
    I remain what I was then
In each essential feature
    Of the fantasies of men.


Yet I note the little chisel
10      Of never-napping Time
Defacing wan and grizzel
    The blazon of my prime.
When at night he thinks me sleeping
    I feel him boring sly
15  Within my bones, and heaping
    Quaintest pains for by-and-by.


Still, I'd go the world with Beauty,
    I would laugh with her and sing,
I would shun divinest duty
20      To resume her worshipping.
But she'd scorn my brave endeavour,
    She would not balm the breeze
By murmuring "Thine for ever!"
    As she did upon this leaze.

## "I Look Into My Glass"

I look into my glass,
And view my wasting skin,
And say, "Would God it came to pass
My heart had shrunk as thin!"

5    For then, I, undistrest
By hearts grown cold to me,
Could lonely wait my endless rest
With equanimity.

But Time, to make me grieve,
10   Part steals, lets part abide;
And shakes this fragile frame at eve
With throbbings of noontide.

From
# POEMS OF THE PAST
# AND THE PRESENT

## EMBARCATION

*(Southampton Docks: October 1899)*

Here, where Vespasian's legions struck the sands,
And Cerdic with his Saxons entered in,
And Henry's army leapt afloat to win
Convincing triumphs over neighbour lands,

5   Vaster battalions press for further strands,
To argue in the selfsame bloody mode
Which this late age of thought, and pact, and code,
Still fails to mend.—Now deckward tramp the bands,

Yellow as autumn leaves, alive as spring;
10   And as each host draws out upon the sea
Beyond which lies the tragical To-be,
None dubious of the cause, none murmuring,

Wives, sisters, parents, wave white hands and smile,
As if they knew not that they weep the while.

## DRUMMER HODGE

### I

They throw in Drummer Hodge, to rest
       Uncoffined—just as found:
His landmark is a kopje-crest
       That breaks the veldt around;
5   And foreign constellations west
       Each night above his mound.

## II

Young Hodge the Drummer never knew—
    Fresh from his Wessex home—
The meaning of the broad Karoo,
10    The Bush, the dusty loam,
And why uprose to nightly view
    Strange stars amid the gloam.

## III

Yet portion of that unknown plain
    Will Hodge for ever be;
15  His homely Northern breast and brain
    Grow to some Southern tree,
And strange-eyed constellations reign
    His stars eternally.

## THE SOULS OF THE SLAIN

### I

The thick lids of Night closed upon me
    Alone at the Bill
    Of the Isle by the Race—
Many-caverned, bald, wrinkled of face—
5  And with darkness and silence the spirit was on me
    To brood and be still.

## II

No wind fanned the flats of the ocean,
 Or promontory sides,
 Or the ooze by the strand,
 Or the bent-bearded slope of the land,
Whose base took its rest amid everlong motion
 Of criss-crossing tides.

## III

Soon from out of the Southward seemed nearing
 A whirr, as of wings
 Waved by mighty-vanned flies,
 Or by night-moths of measureless size,
And in softness and smoothness well-nigh beyond hearing
 Of corporal things.

## IV

And they bore to the bluff, and alighted—
 A dim-discerned train
 Of sprites without mould,
 Frameless souls none might touch or might hold—
On the ledge by the turreted lantern, far-sighted
 By men of the main.

## V

And I heard them say "Home!" and I knew them
 For souls of the felled
 On the earth's nether bord
 Under Capricorn, whither they'd warred,
And I neared in my awe, and gave heedfulness to them
 With breathings inheld.

## VI

Then, it seemed, there approached from the northward
    A senior soul-flame
    Of the like filmy hue:
And he met them and spake: "Is it you,
35 O my men?" Said they, "Aye! We bear homeward and
                         hearthward

    To feast on our fame!"

## VII

"I've flown there before you," he said then:
    "Your households are well;
    But—your kin linger less
40 On your glory and war-mightiness
Than on dearer things."—"Dearer?" cried these from the
                         dead then,

    "Of what do they tell?"

## VIII

"Some mothers muse sadly, and murmur
    Your doings as boys—
45     Recall the quaint ways
Of your babyhood's innocent days.
Some pray that, ere dying, your faith had grown firmer,
    And higher your joys.

## IX

"A father broods: 'Would I had set him
50     To some humble trade,
    And so slacked his high fire,
And his passionate martial desire;
And told him no stories to woo him and whet him
    To this dire crusade!' "

## X

<sup>55</sup> "And, General, how hold out our sweethearts,
    Sworn loyal as doves?"
        —"Many mourn; many think
    It is not unattractive to prink
Them in sables for heroes. Some fickle and fleet hearts
<sup>60</sup>    Have found them new loves."


## XI

"And our wives?" quoth another resignedly,
    "Dwell they on our deeds?"
        —"Deeds of home; that live yet
    Fresh as new—deeds of fondness or fret;
Ancient words that were kindly expressed or unkindly,
    These, these have their heeds."


## XII

—"Alas! then it seems that our glory
    Weighs less in their thought
    Than our old homely acts,
And the long-ago commonplace facts
Of our lives—held by us as scarce part of our story,
    And rated as nought!"


## XIII

Then bitterly some: "Was it wise now
    To raise the tomb-door
        For such knowledge? Away!"
But the rest: "Fame we prized till to-day;
Yet that hearts keep us green for old kindness we prize now
    A thousand times more!"

## XIV

Thus speaking, the trooped apparitions
    Began to disband
    And resolve them in two:
Those whose record was lovely and true
Bore to northward for home: those of bitter traditions
    Again left the land,

## XV

And, towering to seaward in legions,
    They paused at a spot
    Overbending the Race—
That engulphing, ghast, sinister place—
Whither headlong they plunged, to the fathomless regions
    Of myriads forgot.

## XVI

And the spirits of those who were homing
    Passed on, rushingly,
    Like the Pentecost Wind;
And the whirr of their wayfaring thinned
And surceased on the sky, and but left in the gloaming
    Sea-mutterings and me.

## ROME: AT THE PYRAMID OF CESTIUS NEAR THE GRAVES OF SHELLEY AND KEATS

Who, then, was Cestius,
And what is he to me?—
Amid thick thoughts and memories multitudinous
One thought alone brings he.

5    I can recall no word
Of anything he did;
For me he is a man who died and was interred
To leave a pyramid

Whose purpose was exprest
10    Not with its first design,
Nor till, far down in Time, beside it found their rest
Two countrymen of mine.

Cestius in life, maybe,
Slew, breathed out threatening;
15    I know not. This I know: in death all silently
He does a finer thing,

In beckoning pilgrim feet
With marble finger high
To where, by shadowy wall and history-haunted street,
20    Those matchless singers lie. . . .

—Say, then, he lived and died
That stones which bear his name
Should mark, through Time, where two immortal
                Shades abide;
It is an ample fame.

## Zermatt: To the Matterhorn

*(June–July 1897)*

Thirty-two years since, up against the sun,
Seven shapes, thin atomies to lower sight,
Labouringly leapt and gained thy gabled height,
And four lives paid for what the seven had won.

5    They were the first by whom the deed was done,
And when I look at thee, my mind takes flight
To that day's tragic feat of manly might,
As though, till then, of history thou hadst none.

Yet ages ere men topped thee, late and soon
10   Thou didst behold the planets lift and lower;
Saw'st, maybe, Joshua's pausing sun and moon,
And the betokening sky when Cæsar's power
Approached its bloody end; yea, even that Noon
When darkness filled the earth till the ninth hour.

## To an Unborn Pauper Child

### I

Breathe not, hid Heart: cease silently,
And though thy birth-hour beckons thee,
   Sleep the long sleep:
   The Doomsters heap
5   Travails and teens around us here,
And Time-wraiths turn our songsingings to fear.

## II

Hark, how the peoples surge and sigh,
And laughters fail, and greetings die:
    Hopes dwindle; yea,
      Faiths waste away,
Affections and enthusiasms numb;
Thou canst not mend these things if thou dost come.

## III

Had I the ear of wombèd souls
Ere their terrestrial chart unrolls,
    And thou wert free
    To cease, or be,
Then would I tell thee all I know,
And put it to thee: Wilt thou take Life so?

## IV

Vain vow! No hint of mine may hence
To theeward fly: to thy locked sense
    Explain none can
    Life's pending plan:
Thou wilt thy ignorant entry make
Though skies spout fire and blood and nations quake.

## V

Fain would I, dear, find some shut plot
Of earth's wide wold for thee, where not
    One tear, one qualm,
    Should break the calm.
But I am weak as thou and bare;
No man can change the common lot to rare.

Must come and bide. And such are we—
Unreasoning, sanguine, visionary—
    That I can hope
    Health, love, friends, scope
35  In full for thee; can dream thou wilt find
Joys seldom yet attained by humankind!

## TO LIZBIE BROWNE

### I

Dear Lizbie Browne,
Where are you now?
In sun, in rain?—
Or is your brow
5  Past joy, past pain,
Dear Lizbie Browne?

### II

Sweet Lizbie Browne,
How you could smile,
How you could sing!—
10  How archly wile
In glance-giving,
Sweet Lizbie Browne!

### III

And, Lizbie Browne,
Who else had hair
15  Bay-red as yours,
Or flesh so fair
Bred out of doors,
Sweet Lizbie Browne?

### IV

When, Lizbie Browne,
20  You had just begun
To be endeared
By stealth to one,
You disappeared,
My Lizbie Browne!

### V

25  Ay, Lizbie Browne,
So swift your life,
And mine so slow,
You were a wife
Ere I could show
30  Love, Lizbie Browne.

### VI

Still, Lizbie Browne,
You won, they said,
The best of men
When you were wed. . . .
35  Where went you then,
O Lizbie Browne?

## VII

Dear Lizbie Browne,
I should have thought,
"Girls ripen fast,"
40 And coaxed and caught
You ere you passed,
Dear Lizbie Browne!

## VIII

But, Lizbie Browne,
I let you slip;
45 Shaped not a sign;
Touched never your lip
With lip of mine,
Lost Lizbie Browne!

## IX

So, Lizbie Browne,
50 When on a day
Men speak of me
As not, you'll say,
"And who was he?"—
Yes, Lizbie Browne!

## "I Need Not Go"

I need not go
Through sleet and snow
To where I know
She waits for me;
5    She will tarry me there
Till I find it fair,
And have time to spare
From company.

When I've overgot
10    The world somewhat,
When things cost not
Such stress and strain,
Is soon enough
By cypress sough
15    To tell my Love
I am come again.

And if some day,
When none cries nay,
I still delay
20    To seek her side,
(Though ample measure
Of fitting leisure
Await my pleasure)
She will not chide.

25    What—not upbraid me
That I delayed me,
Nor ask what stayed me
So long? Ah, no!—

New cares may claim me,
30 New loves inflame me,
She will not blame me,
But suffer it so.

## At a Hasty Wedding

If hours be years the twain are blest,
For now they solace swift desire
By bonds of every bond the best,
If hours be years. The twain are blest
5 Do eastern stars slope never west,
Nor pallid ashes follow fire:
If hours be years the twain are blest,
For now they solace swift desire.

## His Immortality

I

I saw a dead man's finer part
Shining within each faithful heart
Of those bereft. Then said I: "This must be
His immortality."

## II

I looked there as the seasons wore,
And still his soul continuously bore
A life in theirs. But less its shine excelled
    Than when I first beheld.

## III

His fellow-yearsmen passed, and then
In later hearts I looked for him again;
And found him—shrunk, alas! into a thin
    And spectral mannikin.

## IV

Lastly I ask—now old and chill—
If aught of him remain unperished still;
And find, in me alone, a feeble spark,
    Dying amid the dark.


## WIVES IN THE SERE

### I

Never a careworn wife but shows,
    If a joy suffuse her,
Something beautiful to those
    Patient to peruse her,
Some one charm the world unknows
    Precious to a muser,
Haply what, ere years were foes,
    Moved her mate to choose her.

## II

But, be it a hint of rose
<sub>10</sub>       That an instant hues her,
Or some early light or pose
        Wherewith thought renews her—
Seen by him at full, ere woes
        Practised to abuse her—
<sub>15</sub> Sparely comes it, swiftly goes,
        Time again subdues her.


## An August Midnight

### I

A shaded lamp and a waving blind,
And the beat of a clock from a distant floor:
On this scene enter—winged, horned, and spined—
A longlegs, a moth, and a dumbledore;
<sub>5</sub>  While 'mid my page there idly stands
A sleepy fly, that rubs its hands . . .


### II

Thus meet we five, in this still place,
At this point of time, at this point in space.
—My guests besmear my new-penned line,
<sub>10</sub> Or bang at the lamp and fall supine.
"God's humblest, they!" I muse. Yet why?
They know Earth-secrets that know not I.

## Winter in Durnover Field

SCENE.—A wide stretch of fallow ground recently sown with wheat, and frozen to iron hardness. Three large birds walking about thereon, and wistfully eyeing the surface. Wind keen from north-east: sky a dull grey.

| | |
|---|---|
| ROOK.— | Throughout the field I find no grain; |
| | The cruel frost encrusts the cornland! |
| STARLING.— | Aye: patient pecking now is vain |
| | Throughout the field, I find . . . |
| ROOK.— | No grain! |
| PIGEON.— | Nor will be, comrade, till it rain, |
| | Or genial thawings loose the lorn land |
| | Throughout the field. |
| ROOK.— | I find no grain: |
| | The cruel frost encrusts the cornland! |

## THE LAST CHRYSANTHEMUM

Why should this flower delay so long
    To show its tremulous plumes?
Now is the time of plaintive robin-song,
    When flowers are in their tombs.

5    Through the slow summer, when the sun
    Called to each frond and whorl
That all he could for flowers was being done,
    Why did it not uncurl?

It must have felt that fervid call
10    Although it took no heed,
Waking but now, when leaves like corpses fall,
    And saps all retrocede.

Too late its beauty, lonely thing,
    The season's shine is spent,
15  Nothing remains for it but shivering
    In tempests turbulent.

Had it a reason for delay,
    Dreaming in witlessness
That for a bloom so delicately gay
20    Winter would stay its stress?

—I talk as if the thing were born
    With sense to work its mind;
Yet it is but one mask of many worn
    By the Great Face behind.

## THE DARKLING THRUSH

I leant upon a coppice gate
    When Frost was spectre-gray,
And Winter's dregs made desolate
    The weakening eye of day.
5  The tangled bine-stems scored the sky
    Like strings of broken lyres,
And all mankind that haunted nigh
    Had sought their household fires.

The land's sharp features seemed to be
10      The Century's corpse outleant,
His crypt the cloudy canopy,
    The wind his death-lament.
The ancient pulse of germ and birth
    Was shrunken hard and dry,
15  And every spirit upon earth
    Seemed fervourless as I.

At once a voice arose among
    The bleak twigs overhead
In a full-hearted evensong
20      Of joy illimited;
An aged thrush, frail, gaunt, and small,
    In blast-beruffled plume,
Had chosen thus to fling his soul
    Upon the growing gloom.

25  So little cause for carolings
    Of such ecstatic sound
Was written on terrestrial things
    Afar or nigh around,

That I could think there trembled through
30      His happy good-night air
Some blessed Hope, whereof he knew
        And I was unaware.

*31 December 1900*

## MAD JUDY

When the hamlet hailed a birth
    Judy used to cry:
When she heard our christening mirth
    She would kneel and sigh.
5   She was crazed, we knew, and we
Humoured her infirmity.

When the daughters and the sons
    Gathered them to wed,
And we like-intending ones
10      Danced till dawn was red,
She would rock and mutter, "More
Comers to this stony shore!"

When old Headsman Death laid hands
    On a babe or twain,
15  She would feast, and by her brands
    Sing her songs again.
What she liked we let her do,
Judy was insane, we knew.

## THE RUINED MAID

"O 'Melia, my dear, this does everything crown!
Who could have supposed I should meet you in Town?
And whence such fair garments, such prosperi-ty?"—
"O didn't you know I'd been ruined?" said she.

5    —"You left us in tatters, without shoes or socks,
Tired of digging potatoes, and spudding up docks;
And now you've gay bracelets and bright feathers three!"—
"Yes: that's how we dress when we're ruined," said she.

—"At home in the barton you said 'thee' and 'thou,'
10   And 'thik oon,' and 'theäs oon,' and 't'other'; but now
Your talking quite fits 'ee for high compa-ny!"—
"A polish is gained with one's ruin," said she.

—"Your hands were like paws then, your face blue and
                                                    bleak,
But now I'm bewitched by your delicate cheek,
15   And your little gloves fit as on any la-dy!"—
"We never do work when we're ruined," said she.

—"You used to call home-life a hag-ridden dream,
And you'd sigh, and you'd sock; but at present you seem
To know not of megrims or melancho-ly!"—
20   "True. One's pretty lively when ruined," said she.

—"I wish I had feathers, a fine sweeping gown,
And a delicate face, and could strut about Town!"—
"My dear—a raw country girl, such as you be,
Cannot quite expect that. You ain't ruined," said she.

## THE RESPECTABLE BURGHER
*on "the Higher Criticism"*

Since Reverend Doctors now declare
That clerks and people must prepare
To doubt if Adam ever were;
To hold the flood a local scare;
5    To argue, though the stolid stare,
That everything had happened ere
The prophets to its happening sware;
That David was no giant-slayer,
Nor one to call a God-obeyer
10   In certain details we could spare,
But rather was a debonair
Shrewd bandit, skilled as banjo-player:
That Solomon sang the fleshly Fair,
And gave the Church no thought whate'er,
15   That Esther with her royal wear,
And Mordecai, the son of Jair,
And Joshua's triumphs, Job's despair,
And Balaam's ass's bitter blare;
Nebuchadnezzar's furnace-flare,
20   And Daniel and the den affair,
And other stories rich and rare,
Were writ to make old doctrine wear
Something of a romantic air:
That the Nain widow's only heir,
25   And Lazarus with cadaverous glare
(As done in oils by Piombo's care)
Did not return from Sheol's lair:
That Jael set a fiendish snare,
That Pontius Pilate acted square,
30   That never a sword cut Malchus' ear;
And (but for shame I must forbear)

That ———— ———— did not reappear! . . .
—Since thus they hint, nor turn a hair,
All churchgoing will I forswear,
35 And sit on Sundays in my chair,
And read that moderate man Voltaire.


## THE SELF-UNSEEING

Here is the ancient floor,
Footworn and hollowed and thin,
Here was the former door
Where the dead feet walked in.

5 She sat here in her chair,
Smiling into the fire;
He who played stood there,
Bowing it higher and higher.

Childlike, I danced in a dream;
10 Blessings emblazoned that day;
Everything glowed with a gleam;
Yet we were looking away!

## In Tenebris I

*"Percussus sum sicut fœnum, et aruit cor meum."*—Psalms 101

Wintertime nighs;
But my bereavement-pain
It cannot bring again:
    Twice no one dies.

5    Flower-petals flee;
But, since it once hath been,
No more that severing scene
    Can harrow me.

Birds faint in dread:
10   I shall not lose old strength
In the lone frost's black length:
    Strength long since fled!

Leaves freeze to dun;
But friends can not turn cold
15   This season as of old
    For him with none.

Tempests may scath;
But love can not make smart
Again this year his heart
20   Who no heart hath.

Black is night's cope;
But death will not appal
One who, past doubtings all,
    Waits in unhope.

From
# TIME'S LAUGHINGSTOCKS
## AND OTHER VERSES

# A Trampwoman's Tragedy

## I

From Wynyard's Gap the livelong day,
    The livelong day,
We beat afoot the northward way
    We had travelled times before.
5  The sun-blaze burning on our backs,
Our shoulders sticking to our packs,
By fosseway, fields, and turnpike tracks
    We skirted sad Sedge-Moor.

## II

Full twenty miles we jaunted on,
10      We jaunted on,—
My fancy-man, and jeering John,
    And Mother Lee, and I.
And, as the sun drew down to west,
We climbed the toilsome Poldon crest,
15  And saw, of landskip sights the best,
    The inn that beamed thereby.

## III

For months we had padded side by side,
    Ay, side by side
Through the Great Forest, Blackmoor wide,
20    And where the Parret ran.
We'd faced the gusts on Mendip ridge,
Had crossed the Yeo unhelped by bridge,
Been stung by every Marshwood midge,
    I and my fancy-man.

### IV

25   Lone inns we loved, my man and I,
        My man and I;
"King's Stag," "Windwhistle" high and dry,
       "The Horse" on Hintock Green,
The cosy house at Wynyard's Gap,
30  "The Hut" renowned on Bredy Knap,
And many another wayside tap
      Where folk might sit unseen.

### V

Now as we trudged—O deadly day,
      O deadly day!—
35  I teased my fancy-man in play
      And wanton idleness.
I walked alongside jeering John,
I laid his hand my waist upon;
I would not bend my glances on
40      My lover's dark distress.

### VI

Thus Poldon top at last we won,
      At last we won,
And gained the inn at sink of sun
      Far-famed as "Marshal's Elm."
45  Beneath us figured tor and lea,
From Mendip to the western sea—
I doubt if finer sight there be
      Within this royal realm.

## VII

Inside the settle all a-row—
     All four a-row
We sat, I next to John, to show
     That he had wooed and won.
And then he took me on his knee,
And swore it was his turn to be
My favoured mate, and Mother Lee
     Passed to my former one.

## VIII

Then in a voice I had never heard,
     I had never heard,
My only Love to me: "One word,
     My lady, if you please!
Whose is the child you are like to bear?—
*His?* After all my months o' care?"
God knows 'twas not! But, O despair!
     I nodded—still to tease.

## IX

Then up he sprung, and with his knife—
     And with his knife
He let out jeering Johnny's life,
     Yes; there, at set of sun.
The slant ray through the window nigh
Gilded John's blood and glazing eye,
Ere scarcely Mother Lee and I
     Knew that the deed was done.

## X

The taverns tell the gloomy tale,
    The gloomy tale,
75 How that at Ivel-chester jail
    My Love, my sweetheart swung;
Though stained till now by no misdeed
Save one horse ta'en in time o' need;
(Blue Jimmy stole right many a steed
80     Ere his last fling he flung.)


## XI

Thereaft I walked the world alone,
    Alone, alone!
On his death-day I gave my groan
    And dropt his dead-born child.
85 'Twas nigh the jail, beneath a tree,
None tending me; for Mother Lee
Had died at Glaston, leaving me
    Unfriended on the wild.


## XII

And in the night as I lay weak,
90     As I lay weak,
The leaves a-falling on my cheek,
    The red moon low declined—
The ghost of him I'd die to kiss
Rose up and said: "Ah, tell me this!
95 Was the child mine, or was it his?
    Speak, that I rest may find!"

## XIII

O doubt not but I told him then,
  I told him then,
That I had kept me from all men
  Since we joined lips and swore.
Whereat he smiled, and thinned away
As the wind stirred to call up day . . .
—'Tis past! And here alone I stray
  Haunting the Western Moor.


## THE HOUSE OF HOSPITALITIES

Here we broached the Christmas barrel,
  Pushed up the charred log-ends;
Here we sang the Christmas carol,
    And called in friends.

Time has tired me since we met here
  When the folk now dead were young,
Since the viands were outset here
    And quaint songs sung.

And the worm has bored the viol
  That used to lead the tune,
Rust eaten out the dial
    That struck night's noon.

Now no Christmas brings in neighbours,
  And the New Year comes unlit;
Where we sang the mole now labours,
    And spiders knit.

Yet at midnight if here walking,
   When the moon sheets wall and tree,
I see forms of old time talking,
20       Who smile on me.


## The Rejected Member's Wife

We shall see her no more
    On the balcony,
Smiling, while hurt, at the roar
    As of surging sea
5 From the stormy sturdy band
    Who have doomed her lord's cause,
Though she waves her little hand
    As it were applause.

Here will be candidates yet,
10    And candidates' wives,
Fervid with zeal to set
    Their ideals on our lives:
Here will come market-men
    On the market-days,
15 Here will clash now and then
    More such party assays.

And the balcony will fill
    When such times are renewed,
And the throng in the street will thrill
20    With to-day's mettled mood;
But she will no more stand
    In the sunshine there,
With that wave of her white-gloved hand,
    And that chestnut hair.

## SHUT OUT THAT MOON

Close up the casement, draw the blind,
    Shut out that stealing moon,
She wears too much the guise she wore
    Before our lutes were strewn
With years-deep dust, and names we read
    On a white stone were hewn.

Step not forth on the dew-dashed lawn
    To view the Lady's Chair,
Immense Orion's glittering form,
    The Less and Greater Bear:
Stay in; to such sights we were drawn
    When faded ones were fair.

Brush not the bough for midnight scents
    That come forth lingeringly,
And wake the same sweet sentiments
    They breathed to you and me
When living seemed a laugh, and love
    All it was said to be.

Within the common lamp-lit room
    Prison my eyes and thought;
Let dingy details crudely loom,
    Mechanic speech be wrought:
Too fragrant was Life's early bloom,
    Too tart the fruit it brought!

## The Division

Rain on the windows, creaking doors,
    With blasts that besom the green,
And I am here, and you are there,
    And a hundred miles between!

5  O were it but the weather, Dear,
    O were it but the miles
That summed up all our severance,
    There might be room for smiles.

But that thwart thing betwixt us twain,
10    Which nothing cleaves or clears,
Is more than distance, Dear, or rain,
    And longer than the years!


## "I Say I'll Seek Her"

I say, "I'll seek her side
    Ere hindrance interposes";
    But eve in midnight closes,
And here I still abide.

5  When darkness wears I see
    Her sad eyes in a vision;
    They ask, "What indecision
Detains you, Love, from me?—

"The creaking hinge is oiled,
10    I have unbarred the backway,
    But you tread not the trackway;
And shall the thing be spoiled?

"Far cockcrows echo shrill,
        The shadows are abating,
        And I am waiting, waiting;
But O, you tarry still!"


## "IN THE NIGHT SHE CAME"

I told her when I left one day
That whatsoever weight of care
Might strain our love, Time's mere assault
        Would work no changes there.
And in the night she came to me,
        Toothless, and wan, and old,
With leaden concaves round her eyes,
        And wrinkles manifold.

I tremblingly exclaimed to her,
"O wherefore do you ghost me thus!
I have said that dull defacing Time
        Will bring no dreads to us."
"And is that true of *you?*" she cried
        In voice of troubled tune.
I faltered: "Well . . . I did not think
        You would test me quite so soon!"

She vanished with a curious smile,
Which told me, plainlier than by word,
That my staunch pledge could scarce beguile
        The fear she had averred.
Her doubts then wrought their shape in me,
        And when next day I paid
My due caress, we seemed to be
        Divided by some shade.

# THE NIGHT OF THE DANCE

The cold moon hangs to the sky by its horn,
    And centres its gaze on me;
The stars, like eyes in reverie,
Their westering as for a while forborne,
5    Quiz downward curiously.

Old Robert draws the backbrand in,
    The green logs steam and spit;
The half-awakened sparrows flit
From the riddled thatch; and owls begin
10    To whoo from the gable-slit.

Yes; far and nigh things seem to know
    Sweet scenes are impending here;
That all is prepared; that the hour is near
For welcomes, fellowships, and flow
15    Of sally, song, and cheer;

That spigots are pulled and viols strung;
    That soon will arise the sound
Of measures trod to tunes renowned;
That She will return in Love's low tongue
20    My vows as we wheel around.

# AT CASTERBRIDGE FAIR

## I. The Ballad-Singer

Sing, Ballad-singer, raise a hearty tune;
Make me forget that there was ever a one
I walked with in the meek light of the moon
    When the day's work was done.

Rhyme, Ballad-rhymer, start a country song;
Make me forget that she whom I loved well
Swore she would love me dearly, love me long,
    Then—what I cannot tell!

Sing, Ballad-singer, from your little book;
Make me forget those heart-breaks, achings, fears;
Make me forget her name, her sweet sweet look—
    Make me forget her tears.

## II. Former Beauties

These market-dames, mid-aged, with lips thin-drawn,
    And tissues sere,
Are they the ones we loved in years agone,
    And courted here?

Are these the muslined pink young things to whom
    We vowed and swore
In nooks on summer Sundays by the Froom,
    Or Budmouth shore?

Do they remember those gay tunes we trod
    Clasped on the green;
Aye; trod till moonlight set on the beaten sod
    A satin sheen?

They must forget, forget! They cannot know
    What once they were,
15  Or memory would transfigure them, and show
    Them always fair.


## III. AFTER THE CLUB-DANCE

Black'on frowns east on Maidon,
  And westward to the sea,
But on neither is his frown laden
  With scorn, as his frown on me!

5  At dawn my heart grew heavy,
  I could not sip the wine,
I left the jocund bevy
  And that young man o' mine.

The roadside elms pass by me,—
10  Why do I sink with shame
When the birds a-perch there eye me?
  They, too, have done the same!


## IV. THE MARKET-GIRL

Nobody took any notice of her as she stood on the causey
    kerb,
All eager to sell her honey and apples and bunches of garden
    herb;
And if she had offered to give her wares and herself with
    them too that day,
I doubt if a soul would have cared to take a bargain so choice
    away.

5   But chancing to trace her sunburnt grace that morning as I
                                                        passed nigh,
    I went and I said "Poor maidy dear!—and will none of the
                                                        people buy?"
    And so it began; and soon we knew what the end of it all
                                                        must be,
    And I found that though no others had bid, a prize had been
                                                        won by me.

## V. The Inquiry

And are ye one of Hermitage—
Of Hermitage, by Ivel Road,
And do ye know, in Hermitage
A thatch-roofed house where sengreens grow?
5   And does John Waywood live there still—
He of the name that there abode
When father hurdled on the hill
        Some fifteen years ago?

Does he now speak o' Patty Beech,
10  The Patty Beech he used to—see,
Or ask at all if Patty Beech
Is known or heard of out this way?
—Ask ever if she's living yet,
And where her present home may be,
15  And how she bears life's fag and fret
        After so long a day?

In years agone at Hermitage
This faded face was counted fair,
None fairer; and at Hermitage
20  We swore to wed when he should thrive.
But never a chance had he or I,
And waiting made his wish outwear,
And Time, that dooms man's love to die,
        Preserves a maid's alive.

## VI. A Wife Waits

Will's at the dance in the Club-room below,
    Where the tall liquor-cups foam;
I on the pavement up here by the Bow,
    Wait, wait, to steady him home.

5    Will and his partner are treading a tune,
        Loving companions they be;
Willy, before we were married in June,
        Said he loved no one but me;

Said he would let his old pleasures all go
10    Ever to live with his Dear.
Will's at the dance in the Club-room below,
    Shivering I wait for him here.

## VII. After the Fair

The singers are gone from the Cornmarket-place
    With their broadsheets of rhymes,
The street rings no longer in treble and bass
    With their skits on the times,
5    And the Cross, lately thronged, is a dim naked space
    That but echoes the stammering chimes.

From Clock-corner steps, as each quarter ding-dongs,
    Away the folk roam
By the "Hart" and Grey's Bridge into byways and "drongs,"
10    Or across the ridged loam;
The younger ones shrilling the lately heard songs,
    The old saying, "Would we were home."

The shy-seeming maiden so mute in the fair
        Now rattles and talks,
And that one who looked the most swaggering there
        Grows sad as she walks,
And she who seemed eaten by cankering care
        In statuesque sturdiness stalks.

And midnight clears High Street of all but the ghosts
        Of its buried burghees,
From the latest far back to those old Roman hosts
        Whose remains one yet sees,
Who loved, laughed, and fought, hailed their friends, drank
                                        their toasts
    At their meeting-times here, just as these!


## To Carrey Clavel

You turn your back, you turn your back,
        And never your face to me,
Alone you take your homeward track,
        And scorn my company.

What will you do when Charley's seen
        Dewbeating down this way?
—You'll turn your back as now, you mean?
        Nay, Carrey Clavel, nay!

You'll see none's looking; put your lip
        Up like a tulip, so;
And he will coll you, bend, and sip:
        Yes, Carrey, yes; I know!

## THE ORPHANED OLD MAID

*I* wanted to marry, but father said, "No—
'Tis weakness in women to give themselves so;
If you care for your freedom you'll listen to me,
Make a spouse in your pocket, and let the men be."

5  I spake on't again and again: father cried,
"Why—if you go husbanding, where shall I bide?
For never a home's for me elsewhere than here!"
And I yielded; for father had ever been dear.

But now father's gone, and I feel growing old,
10  And I'm lonely and poor in this house on the wold,
And my sweetheart that was found a partner elsewhere,
And nobody flings me a thought or a care.


## ROSE-ANN

Why didn't you say you was promised, Rose-Ann?
   Why didn't you name it to me,
Ere ever you tempted me hither, Rose-Ann,
   So often, so wearifully?

5  O why did you let me be near 'ee, Rose-Ann,
   Talking things about wedlock so free,
And never by nod or by whisper, Rose-Ann,
   Give a hint that it wasn't to be?

Down home I was raising a flock of stock ewes,
10   Cocks and hens, and wee chickens by scores,
And lavendered linen all ready to use,
   A-dreaming that they would be yours.

Mother said: "She's a sport-making maiden, my son";
And a pretty sharp quarrel had we;
O why do you prove by this wrong you have done
That I saw not what mother could see?

Never once did you say you was promised, Rose-Ann,
Never once did I dream it to be;
And it cuts to the heart to be treated, Rose-Ann,
As you in your scorning treat me!


## THE HOMECOMING

*Gruffly growled the wind on Toller downland broad and bare,*
*And lonesome was the house, and dark; and few came there.*

"Now don't ye rub your eyes so red; we're home and have
no cares;
Here's a skimmer-cake for supper, peckled onions, and some
pears;
I've got a little keg o' summat strong, too, under stairs:
—What, slight your husband's victuals? Other brides can
tackle theirs!"

*The wind of winter mooed and mouthed their chimney like a horn,*
*And round the house and past the house 'twas leafless and lorn.*

"But my dear and tender poppet, then, how came ye to
agree
In Ivel church this morning? Sure, thereright you married
me!"
—"Hoo-hoo!—I don't know—I forgot how strange and far
'twould be,
An' I wish I was at home again with dear daddee!"

*Gruffly growled the wind on Toller downland broad and bare,*
*And lonesome was the house, and dark; and few came there.*

15 "I didn't think such furniture as this was all you'd own,
  And great black beams for ceiling, and a floor o' wretched
                                          stone,
  And nasty pewter platters, horrid forks of steel and bone,
  And a monstrous crock in chimney. 'Twas to me quite
                                          unbeknown!"

*Rattle rattle went the door; down flapped a cloud of smoke,*
20 *As shifting north the wicked wind assayed a smarter stroke.*

  "Now sit ye by the fire, poppet; put yourself at ease:
  And keep your little thumb out of your mouth, dear, please!
  And I'll sing to 'ee a pretty song of lovely flowers and bees,
  And happy lovers taking walks within a grove o' trees."

25 *Gruffly growled the wind on Toller Down, so bleak and bare,*
  *And lonesome was the house, and dark; and few came there.*

  "Now, don't ye gnaw your handkercher; 'twill hurt your
                                          little tongue,
  And if you do feel spitish, 'tis because ye are over young;
  But you'll be getting older, like us all, ere very long,
30 And you'll see me as I am—a man who never did 'ee
                                          wrong."

*Straight from Whit'sheet Hill to Benvill Lane the blusters pass,*
*Hitting hedges, milestones, handposts, trees, and tufts of grass.*

  "Well, had I only known, my dear, that this was how you'd
                                          be,
  I'd have married her of riper years that was so fond of me.
35 But since I can't, I've half a mind to run away to sea,
  And leave 'ee to go barefoot to your d——d daddee!"

*Up one wall and down the other—past each window-pane—*
*Prance the gusts, and then away down Crimmercrock's long lane.*


"I—I—don't know what to say to't, since your wife I've
vowed to be;
And as 'tis done, I s'pose here I must bide—poor me!
Aye—as you are ki-ki-kind, I'll try to live along with 'ee,
Although I'd fain have stayed at home with dear daddee!"


*Gruffly growled the wind on Toller Down, so bleak and bare,*
*And lonesome was the house, and dark; and few came there.*


"That's right, my Heart! And though on haunted Toller
Down we be,
And the wind swears things in chimley, we'll to supper
merrily!
So don't ye tap your shoe so pettish-like; but smile at me,
And ye'll soon forget to sock and sigh for dear daddee!"


A CHURCH ROMANCE
*(Mellstock circa 1835)*

She turned in the high pew, until her sight
Swept the west gallery, and caught its row
Of music-men with viol, book, and bow
Against the sinking sad tower-window light.


She turned again; and in her pride's despite
One strenuous viol's inspirer seemed to throw
A message from his string to her below,
Which said: "I claim thee as my own forthright!"

Thus their hearts' bond began, in due time signed.
10 And long years thence, when Age had scared Romance,
At some old attitude of his or glance
That gallery-scene would break upon her mind,
With him as minstrel, ardent, young, and trim,
Bowing "New Sabbath" or "Mount Ephraim".


## AFTER THE LAST BREATH
*(J.H. 1813–1904)*

There's no more to be done, or feared, or hoped;
None now need watch, speak low, and list, and tire;
No irksome crease outsmoothed, no pillow sloped
    Does she require.

5 Blankly we gaze. We are free to go or stay;
Our morrow's anxious plans have missed their aim;
Whether we leave to-night or wait till day
    Counts as the same.

The lettered vessels of medicaments
10 Seem asking wherefore we have set them here;
Each palliative its silly face presents
    As useless gear.

And yet we feel that something savours well;
We note a numb relief withheld before;
15 Our well-beloved is prisoner in the cell
    Of Time no more.

We see by littles now the deft achievement
Whereby she has escaped the Wrongers all,
In view of which our momentary bereavement
20     Outshapes but small.

*1904*

ONE WE KNEW
*(M.H. 1772–1857)*

She told how they used to form for the country dances—
    "The Triumph," "The New-rigged Ship"—
To the light of the guttering wax in the panelled manses,
    And in cots to the blink of a dip.

5  She spoke of the wild "poussetting" and "allemanding"
    On carpet, on oak, and on sod;
And the two long rows of ladies and gentlemen standing,
    And the figures the couples trod.

She showed us the spot where the maypole was yearly
                       planted,
10    And where the bandsmen stood
While breeched and kerchiefed partners whirled, and panted
    To choose each other for good.

She told of that far-back day when they learnt astounded
    Of the death of the King of France:
15  Of the Terror; and then of Bonaparte's unbounded
    Ambition and arrogance.

Of how his threats woke warlike preparations
    Along the southern strand,
And how each night brought tremors and trepidations
20    Lest morning should see him land.

She said she had often heard the gibbet creaking
    As it swayed in the lightning flash,
Had caught from the neighbouring town a small child's
                     shrieking
    At the cart-tail under the lash. . . .

25 With cap-framed face and long gaze into the embers—
        We seated around her knees—
She would dwell on such dead themes, not as one who
                                    remembers,
        But rather as one who sees.

She seemed one left behind of a band gone distant
30      So far that no tongue could hail:
Past things retold were to her as things existent,
        Things present but as a tale.


### She Hears the Storm

There was a time in former years—
        While my roof-tree was his—
When I should have been distressed by fears
        At such a night as this!

5   I should have murmured anxiously,
        "The pricking rain strikes cold;
His road is bare of hedge or tree,
        And he is getting old."

But now the fitful chimney-roar,
10      The drone of Thorncombe trees,
The Froom in flood upon the moor,
        The mud of Mellstock Leaze,

The candle slanting sooty-wick'd,
        The thuds upon the thatch,
15  The eaves-drops on the window flicked,
        The clacking garden-hatch,

And what they mean to wayfarers,
      I scarcely heed or mind;
He has won that storm-tight roof of hers
      Which Earth grants all her kind.


## The Man He Killed

      "Had he and I but met
      By some old ancient inn,
We should have sat us down to wet
      Right many a nipperkin!

      "But ranged as infantry,
      And staring face to face,
I shot at him as he at me,
      And killed him in his place.

      "I shot him dead because—
      Because he was my foe,
Just so: my foe of course he was;
      That's clear enough; although

      "He thought he'd 'list, perhaps,
      Off-hand like—just as I—
Was out of work—had sold his traps—
      No other reason why.

      "Yes; quaint and curious war is!
      You shoot a fellow down
You'd treat if met where any bar is,
      Or help to half-a-crown."

*1902*

63

# One Ralph Blossom Soliloquizes

("It being deposed that vij women who were mayds before he
knew them have been brought upon the towne [rates?] by the
fornications of one Ralph Blossom, Mr. Maior inquired why he
should not contribute xiv pence weekly toward their mayntenance.
But it being shewn that the sayd R.B. was dying of a purple feaver,
no order was made."—*Budmouth Borough Minutes: 16–*)

When I am in hell or some such place,
A-groaning over my sorry case,
What will those seven women say to me
Who, when I coaxed them, answered "Aye" to me?

5    "I did not understand your sign!"
Will be the words of Caroline;
While Jane will cry, "If I'd had proof of you,
I should have learnt to hold aloof of you!"

"I won't reproach: it was to be!"
10   Will drily murmur Cicely;
And Rosa: "I feel no hostility,
For I must own I lent facility."

Lizzy says: "Sharp was my regret,
And sometimes it is now! But yet
15   I joy that, though it brought notoriousness,
I knew Love once and all its gloriousness!"

Says Patience: "Why are we apart?
Small harm did you, my poor Sweet Heart!
A manchild born, now tall and beautiful,
20   Was worth the ache of days undutiful."

And Anne cries: "O the time was fair,
So wherefore should you burn down there?
There is a deed under the sun, my Love,
and that was ours. What's done is done, my Love.
These trumpets here in Heaven are dumb to me
With you away. Dear, come, O come to me!"

From
SATIRES OF
CIRCUMSTANCE,
LYRICS AND
REVERIES

## CHANNEL FIRING

That night your great guns, unawares,
Shook all our coffins as we lay,
And broke the chancel window-squares,
We thought it was the Judgment-day

And sat upright. While drearisome
Arose the howl of wakened hounds:
The mouse let fall the altar-crumb,
The worms drew back into the mounds,

The glebe cow drooled. Till God called, "No;
It's gunnery practice out at sea
Just as before you went below;
The world is as it used to be:

"All nations striving strong to make
Red war yet redder. Mad as hatters
They do no more for Christés sake
Than you who are helpless in such matters.

"That this is not the judgment-hour
For some of them's a blessed thing,
For if it were they'd have to scour
Hell's floor for so much threatening. . . .

"Ha, ha. It will be warmer when
I blow the trumpet (if indeed
I ever do; for you are men,
And rest eternal sorely need)."

So down we lay again. "I wonder,
Will the world ever saner be,"
Said one, "than when He sent us under
In our indifferent century!"

And many a skeleton shook his head.
30 "Instead of preaching forty year,"
My neighbour Parson Thirdly said,
"I wish I had stuck to pipes and beer."

Again the guns disturbed the hour,
Roaring their readiness to avenge,
35 As far inland as Stourton Tower,
And Camelot, and starlit Stonehenge.

*April 1914*


## THE CONVERGENCE OF THE TWAIN
*(Lines on the loss of the "Titanic")*


I

In a solitude of the sea
Deep from human vanity,
And the Pride of Life that planned her, stilly couches she.


II

Steel chambers, late the pyres
5 Of her salamandrine fires,
Cold currents thrid, and turn to rhythmic tidal lyres.

### III

Over the mirrors meant
To glass the opulent
The sea-worm crawls—grotesque, slimed, dumb, indifferent.


### IV

Jewels in joy designed
To ravish the sensuous mind
Lie lightless, all their sparkles bleared and black and blind.


### V

Dim moon-eyed fishes near
Gaze at the gilded gear
And query: "What does this vaingloriousness down here?" . . .


### VI

Well: while was fashioning
This creature of cleaving wing,
The Immanent Will that stirs and urges everything


### VII

Prepared a sinister mate
For her—so gaily great—
A Shape of Ice, for the time far and dissociate.


### VIII

And as the smart ship grew
In stature, grace, and hue,
In shadowy silent distance grew the Iceberg too.

## IX

25

Alien they seemed to be:
No mortal eye could see
The intimate welding of their later history,

## X

Or sign that they were bent
By paths coincident
On being anon twin halves of one august event,

30

## XI

Till the Spinner of the Years
Said "Now!" And each one hears,
And consummation comes, and jars two hemispheres.

## "MY SPIRIT WILL NOT HAUNT THE MOUND"

My spirit will not haunt the mound
    Above my breast,
But travel, memory-possessed,
To where my tremulous being found
    Life largest, best.

My phantom-footed shape will go
    When nightfall grays
Hither and thither along the ways
I and another used to know
    In backward days.

And there you'll find me, if a jot
        You still should care
For me, and for my curious air;
If otherwise, then I shall not,
15        For you, be there.


WESSEX HEIGHTS

*(1896)*

There are some heights in Wessex, shaped as if by a kindly
                                        hand
For thinking, dreaming, dying on, and at crises when I stand,
Say, on Ingpen Beacon eastward, or on Wylls-Neck
                                        westwardly,
I seem where I was before my birth, and after death may be.

5  In the lowlands I have no comrade, not even the lone man's
                                        friend—
Her who suffereth long and is kind; accepts what he is too
                                        weak to mend:
Down there they are dubious and askance; there nobody
                                        thinks as I,
But mind-chains do not clank where one's next neighbour
                                        is the sky.

In the towns I am tracked by phantoms having weird detec-
                                        tive ways—
10  Shadows of beings who fellowed with myself of earlier days:
They hang about at places, and they say harsh heavy
                                        things—
Men with a wintry sneer, and women with tart disparagings.

Down there I seem to be false to myself, my simple self that
was,
And is not now, and I see him watching, wondering what
crass cause
15  Can have merged him into such a strange continuator as this,
Who yet has something in common with himself, my
chrysalis.


I cannot go to the great grey Plain; there's a figure against
the moon,
Nobody sees it but I, and it makes my breast beat out of
tune;
I cannot go to the tall-spired town, being barred by the forms
now passed
20  For everybody but me, in whose long vision they stand there
fast.


There's a ghost at Yell'ham Bottom chiding loud at the fall
of the night,
There's a ghost in Froom-side Vale, thin-lipped and vague,
in a shroud of white,
There is one in the railway train whenever I do not want it
near,
I see its profile against the pane, saying what I would not
hear.


25  As for one rare fair woman, I am now but a thought of hers,
I enter her mind and another thought succeeds me that she
prefers;
Yet my love for her in its fulness she herself even did not
know;
Well, time cures hearts of tenderness, and now I can let her go.

So I am found on Ingpen Beacon, or on Wylls-Neck to the
                                                    west,
30 Or else on homely Bulbarrow, or little Pilsdon Crest,
Where men have never cared to haunt, nor women have
                                            walked with me,
And ghosts then keep their distance; and I know some
                                                    liberty.


## The Schreckhorn
*(With thoughts of Leslie Stephen)*

Aloof, as if a thing of mood and whim;
Now that its spare and desolate figure gleams
Upon my nearing vision, less it seems
A looming Alp-height than a guise of him
5 Who scaled its horn with ventured life and limb,
Drawn on by vague imaginings, maybe,
Of semblance to his personality
In its quaint glooms, keen lights, and rugged trim.

At his last change, when Life's dull coils unwind,
10 Will he, in old love, hitherward escape,
And the eternal essence of his mind
Enter this silent adamantine shape,
And his low voicing haunt its slipping snows
When dawn that calls the climber dyes them rose?


## "Ah, Are You Digging on My Grave?"

"Ah, are you digging on my grave,
        My loved one?—planting rue?"
—"No: yesterday he went to wed
One of the brightest wealth has bred.
5 'It cannot hurt her now,' he said,
        'That I should not be true.' "

"Then who is digging on my grave?
        My nearest dearest kin?"
—"Ah, no: they sit and think, 'What use!
What good will planting flowers produce?
No tendance of her mound can loose
        Her spirit from Death's gin.' "

"But some one digs upon my grave?
        My enemy?—prodding sly?"
—"Nay: when she heard you had passed the Gate
That shuts on all flesh soon or late,
She thought you no more worth her hate,
        And cares not where you lie."

"Then, who is digging on my grave?
        Say—since I have not guessed!"
—"O it is I, my mistress dear,
Your little dog, who still lives near,
And much I hope my movements here
        Have not disturbed your rest?"

"Ah, yes! *You* dig upon my grave. . . .
        Why flashed it not on me
That one true heart was left behind!
What feeling do we ever find
To equal among human kind
        A dog's fidelity!"

"Mistress, I dug upon your grave
        To bury a bone, in case
I should be hungry near this spot
When passing on my daily trot.
I am sorry, but I quite forgot
        It was your resting-place."

## BEFORE AND AFTER SUMMER

### I

Looking forward to the spring
One puts up with anything.
On this February day
Though the winds leap down the street,
5  Wintry scourgings seem but play,
And these later shafts of sleet
—Sharper pointed than the first—
And these later snows—the worst—
Are as a half-transparent blind
10  Riddled by rays from sun behind.

### II

Shadows of the October pine
Reach into this room of mine:
On the pine there swings a bird;
He is shadowed with the tree.
5  Mutely perched he bills no word;
Blank as I am even is he.
For those happy suns are past,
Fore-discerned in winter last.
When went by their pleasure, then?
10  I, alas, perceived not when.

## At Day-Close in November

The ten hours' light is abating,
  And a late bird wings across,
Where the pines, like waltzers waiting,
  Give their black heads a toss.

5   Beech leaves, that yellow the noon-time,
  Float past like specks in the eye;
I set every tree in my June time,
  And now they obscure the sky.

And the children who ramble through here
10   Conceive that there never has been
A time when no tall trees grew here,
  That none will in time be seen.

# POEMS OF 1912–13
*Veteris vestigia flammae*

## THE GOING

Why did you give no hint that night
That quickly after the morrow's dawn,
And calmly, as if indifferent quite,
You would close your term here, up and be gone
     Where I could not follow
     With wing of swallow
To gain one glimpse of you ever anon!

     Never to bid good-bye,
     Or lip me the softest call,
Or utter a wish for a word, while I
Saw morning harden upon the wall,
     Unmoved, unknowing
     That your great going
Had place that moment, and altered all.

Why do you make me leave the house
And think for a breath it is you I see
At the end of the alley of bending boughs
Where so often at dusk you used to be;
     Till in darkening dankness
     The yawning blankness
Of the perspective sickens me!

     You were she who abode
     By those red-veined rocks far West,
You were the swan-necked one who rode
Along the beetling Beeny Crest,
     And, reining nigh me,
     Would muse and eye me,
While Life unrolled us its very best.

Why, then, latterly did we not speak,
30　Did we not think of those days long dead,
And ere your vanishing strive to seek
That time's renewal? We might have said,
　　"In this bright spring weather
　　We'll visit together
35　Those places that once we visited."

　　Well, well! All's past amend,
　　Unchangeable. It must go.
I seem but a dead man held on end
To sink down soon. . . . O you could not know
40　　That such swift fleeing
　　No soul foreseeing—
Not even I—would undo me so!

*December 1912*


YOUR LAST DRIVE

Here by the moorway you returned,
And saw the borough lights ahead
That lit your face—all undiscerned
To be in a week the face of the dead,
5　And you told of the charm of that haloed view
That never again would beam on you.

And on your left you passed the spot
Where eight days later you were to lie,
And be spoken of as one who was not;
10　Beholding it with a heedless eye
As alien from you, though under its tree
You soon would halt everlastingly.

I drove not with you. . . . Yet had I sat
At your side that eve I should not have seen
That the countenance I was glancing at
Had a last-time look in the flickering sheen,
Nor have read the writing upon your face,
"I go hence soon to my resting-place;

"You may miss me then. But I shall not know
How many times you visit me there,
Or what your thoughts are, or if you go
There never at all. And I shall not care.
Should you censure me I shall take no heed
And even your praises no more shall need."

True: never you'll know. And you will not mind.
But shall I then slight you because of such?
Dear ghost, in the past did you ever find
The thought "What profit," move me much?
Yet abides the fact, indeed, the same,—
You are past love, praise, indifference, blame.

*December 1912*

## THE WALK

You did not walk with me
Of late to the hill-top tree
        By the gated ways,
        As in earlier days;
        You were weak and lame,
        So you never came,
And I went alone, and I did not mind,
Not thinking of you as left behind.

I walked up there to-day
10 Just in the former way;
 Surveyed around
 The familiar ground
 By myself again:
 What difference, then?
15 Only that underlying sense
Of the look of a room on returning thence.


## Rain on a Grave

Clouds spout upon her
 Their waters amain
 In ruthless disdain,—
Her who but lately
5  Had shivered with pain
As at touch of dishonour
If there had lit on her
So coldly, so straightly
 Such arrows of rain:

10 One who to shelter
 Her delicate head
Would quicken and quicken
 Each tentative tread
If drops chanced to pelt her
15  That summertime spills
 In dust-paven rills
When thunder-clouds thicken
 And birds close their bills.

Would that I lay there
  And she were housed here!
Or better, together
Were folded away there
Exposed to one weather
We both,—who would stray there
When sunny the day there,
    Or evening was clear
    At the prime of the year.

Soon will be growing
    Green blades from her mound,
And daisies be showing
    Like stars on the ground,
Till she form part of them—
Ay—the sweet heart of them,
Loved beyond measure
With a child's pleasure
    All her life's round.

*January 31, 1913*


WITHOUT CEREMONY

It was your way, my dear,
To vanish without a word
When callers, friends, or kin
Had left, and I hastened in
To rejoin you, as I inferred.

And when you'd a mind to career
Off anywhere—say to town—
You were all on a sudden gone
Before I had thought thereon,
Or noticed your trunks were down.

So, now that you disappear
For ever in that swift style,
Your meaning seems to me
Just as it used to be:
15   "Good-bye is not worth while!"

## LAMENT

How she would have loved
A party to-day!—
Bright-hatted and gloved,
With table and tray
5  And chairs on the lawn
Her smiles would have shone
With welcomings. . . . But
She is shut, she is shut
    From friendship's spell
10     In the jailing shell
    Of her tiny cell.

Or she would have reigned
At a dinner to-night
With ardours unfeigned,
15  And a generous delight;
All in her abode
She'd have freely bestowed
On her guests. . . . But alas,
She is shut under grass
20     Where no cups flow,
    Powerless to know
    That it might be so.

And she would have sought
With a child's eager glance
25  The shy snowdrops brought
By the new year's advance,
And peered in the rime
Of Candlemas-time
For crocuses . . . chanced
30  It that she were not tranced
     From sights she loved best;
     Wholly possessed
     By an infinite rest!

And we are here staying
35  Amid these stale things
Who care not for gaying,
And those junketings
That used so to joy her,
And never to cloy her
40  As us they cloy! . . . But
She is shut, she is shut
     From the cheer of them, dead
     To all done and said
     In her yew-arched bed.


## THE HAUNTER

He does not think that I haunt here nightly:
     How shall I let him know
That whither his fancy sets him wandering
     I, too, alertly go?—
5  Hover and hover a few feet from him
     Just as I used to do,
But cannot answer the words he lifts me—
     Only listen thereto!

When I could answer he did not say them:
10      When I could let him know
How I would like to join in his journeys
      Seldom he wished to go.
Now that he goes and wants me with him
      More than he used to do,
15  Never he sees my faithful phantom
      Though he speaks thereto.


Yes, I companion him to places
      Only dreamers know,
Where the shy hares print long paces,
20      Where the night rooks go;
Into old aisles where the past is all to him,
      Close as his shade can do,
Always lacking the power to call to him,
      Near as I reach thereto!


25  What a good haunter I am, O tell him!
      Quickly make him know
If he but sigh since my loss befell him
      Straight to his side I go.
Tell him a faithful one is doing
30      All that love can do
Still that his path may be worth pursuing,
      And to bring peace thereto.


## THE VOICE

Woman much missed, how you call to me, call to me,
Saying that now you are not as you were
When you had changed from the one who was all to me,
But as at first, when our day was fair.

Can it be you that I hear? Let me view you, then,
Standing as when I drew near to the town
Where you would wait for me: yes, as I knew you then,
Even to the original air-blue gown!

Or is it only the breeze, in its listlessness
Travelling across the wet mead to me here,
You being ever dissolved to wan wistlessness,
Heard no more again far or near?

Thus I; faltering forward,
Leaves around me falling,
Wind oozing thin through the thorn from norward,
And the woman calling.

*December 1912*


HIS VISITOR

I come across from Mellstock while the moon wastes weaker
To behold where I lived with you for twenty years and
more:
I shall go in the gray, at the passing of the mail-train,
And need no setting open of the long familiar door
As before.

The change I notice in my once own quarters!
A formal-fashioned border where the daisies used to be,
The rooms new painted, and the pictures altered,
And other cups and saucers, and no cosy nook for tea
As with me.

I discern the dim faces of the sleep-wrapt servants;
They are not those who tended me through feeble hours and
                                        strong,
But strangers quite, who never knew my rule here,
Who never saw me painting, never heard my softling song
15          Float along.

So I don't want to linger in this re-decked dwelling,
I feel too uneasy at the contrasts I behold,
And I make again for Mellstock to return here never,
And rejoin the roomy silence, and the mute and manifold
20          Souls of old.

                                        *1913*


## AFTER A JOURNEY

Hereto I come to view a voiceless ghost;
    Whither, O whither will its whim now draw me?
Up the cliff, down, till I'm lonely, lost,
    And the unseen waters' ejaculations awe me.
5  Where you will next be there's no knowing,
        Facing round about me everywhere,
            With your nut-coloured hair,
And gray eyes, and rose-flush coming and going.

Yes: I have re-entered your olden haunts at last;
10      Through the years, through the dead scenes I have tracked
                                        you;
What have you now found to say of our past—
        Scanned across the dark space wherein I have lacked you?
Summer gave us sweets, but autumn wrought division?
        Things were not lastly as firstly well
15          With us twain, you tell?
But all's closed now, despite Time's derision.

I see what you are doing: you are leading me on
    To the spots we knew when we haunted here together,
The waterfall, above which the mist-bow shone
20     At the then fair hour in the then fair weather,
And the cave just under, with a voice still so hollow
    That it seems to call out to me from forty years ago,
        When you were all aglow,
And not the thin ghost that I now frailly follow!

25  Ignorant of what there is flitting here to see,
    The waked birds preen and the seals flop lazily;
Soon you will have, Dear, to vanish from me,
    For the stars close their shutters and the dawn whitens
                                        hazily.
Trust me, I mind not, though Life lours,
30     The bringing me here; nay, bring me here again!
        I am just the same as when
Our days were a joy, and our paths through flowers.

                                        *Pentargan Bay*


## AT CASTLE BOTEREL

As I drive to the junction of lane and highway,
    And the drizzle bedrenches the waggonette,
I look behind at the fading byway,
    And see on its slope, now glistening wet,
5       Distinctly yet

Myself and a girlish form benighted
    In dry March weather. We climb the road
Beside a chaise. We had just alighted
    To ease the sturdy pony's load
10      When he sighed and slowed.

What we did as we climbed, and what we talked of
   Matters not much, nor to what it led,—
Something that life will not be balked of
   Without rude reason till hope is dead,
      And feeling fled.

It filled but a minute. But was there ever
   A time of such quality, since or before,
In that hill's story? To one mind never,
   Though it has been climbed, foot-swift, foot-sore,
      By thousands more.

Primaeval rocks form the road's steep border,
   And much have they faced there, first and last,
Of the transitory in Earth's long order;
   But what they record in colour and cast
      Is—that we two passed.

And to me, though Time's unflinching rigour,
   In mindless rote, has ruled from sight
The substance now, one phantom figure
   Remains on the slope, as when that night
      Saw us alight.

I look and see it there, shrinking, shrinking,
   I look back at it amid the rain
For the very last time; for my sand is sinking,
   And I shall traverse old love's domain
      Never again.

*March 1913*

## "SHE CHARGED ME"

She charged me with having said this and that
To another woman long years before,
In the very parlour where we sat,—

Sat on a night when the endless pour
5  Of rain on the roof and the road below
Bent the spring of the spirit more and more. . . .

—So charged she me; and the Cupid's bow
Of her mouth was hard, and her eyes, and her face,
And her white forefinger lifted slow.

10  Had she done it gently, or shown a trace
That not too curiously would she view
A folly flown ere her reign had place,

A kiss might have closed it. But I knew
From the fall of each word, and the pause between,
15  That the curtain would drop upon us two
Ere long, in our play of slave and queen.


## THE MOON LOOKS IN

### I

I have risen again,
And awhile survey
By my chilly ray
Through your window-pane
5  Your upturned face,
As you think, "Ah—she
Now dreams of me
In her distant place!"

## II

10

I pierce her blind
In her far-off home:
She fixes a comb,
And says in her mind,
"I start in an hour;
Whom shall I meet?

15

Won't the men be sweet,
And the women sour!"

## IN THE DAYS OF CRINOLINE

A plain tilt-bonnet on her head
She took the path across the leaze.
—Her spouse the vicar, gardening, said,
"Too dowdy that, for coquetries,

5

So I can hoe at ease."

But when she had passed into the heath,
And gained the wood beyond the flat,
She raised her skirts, and from beneath
Unpinned and drew as from a sheath

10

An ostrich-feathered hat.

And where the hat had hung she now
Concealed and pinned the dowdy hood,
And set the hat upon her brow,
And thus emerging from the wood

15

Tripped on in jaunty mood.

The sun was low and crimson-faced
As two came that way from the town,
And plunged into the wood untraced. . . .
When severally therefrom they paced
20      The sun had quite gone down.

The hat and feather disappeared,
The dowdy hood again was donned,
And in the gloom the fair one neared
Her home and husband dour, who conned
25      Calmly his blue-eyed blonde.

"To-day," he said, "you have shown good sense,
A dress so modest and so meek
Should always deck your goings hence
Alone." And as a recompense
30      He kissed her on the cheek.


## The Workbox

"See, here's the workbox, little wife,
    That I made of polished oak."
He was a joiner, of village life;
    She came of borough folk.

5   He holds the present up to her
    As with a smile she nears
And answers to the profferer,
    " 'Twill last all my sewing years!"

"I warrant it will. And longer too.
0   'Tis a scantling that I got
Off poor John Wayward's coffin, who
    Died of they knew not what.

"The shingled pattern that seems to cease
      Against your box's rim
15  Continues right on in the piece
      That's underground with him.

"And while I worked it made me think
      Of timber's varied doom;
One inch where people eat and drink,
20     The next inch in a tomb.

"But why do you look so white, my dear,
      And turn aside your face?
You knew not that good lad, I fear,
      Though he came from your native place?"

25  "How could I know that good young man,
      Though he came from my native town,
When he must have left far earlier than
      I was a woman grown?"

"Ah, no. I should have understood!
30     It shocked you that I gave
To you one end of a piece of wood
      Whose other is in a grave?"

"Don't, dear, despise my intellect,
      Mere accidental things
35  Of that sort never have effect
      On my imaginings."

Yet still her lips were limp and wan,
      Her face still held aside,
As if she had known not only John,
40     But known of what he died.

## EXEUNT OMNES

### I

Everybody else, then, going,
And I still left where the fair was? . . .
Much have I seen of neighbour loungers
    Making a lusty showing,
    Each now past all knowing.

### II

There is an air of blankness
In the street and the littered spaces;
Thoroughfare, steeple, bridge and highway
    Wizen themselves to lankness;
    Kennels dribble dankness.

### III

Folk all fade. And whither,
As I wait alone where the fair was?
Into the clammy and numbing night-fog
    Whence they entered hither.
    Soon one more goes thither!

*June 2, 1913*

# SATIRES OF CIRCUMSTANCE IN FIFTEEN GLIMPSES

## I. AT TEA

The kettle descants in a cosy drone,
And the young wife looks in her husband's face,
And then at her guest's, and shows in her own
Her sense that she fills an envied place;
5 And the visiting lady is all abloom,
And says there was never so sweet a room.

And the happy young housewife does not know
That the woman beside her was first his choice,
Till the fates ordained it could not be so. . . .
10 Betraying nothing in look or voice
The guest sits smiling and sips her tea,
And he throws her a stray glance yearningly.

## II. IN CHURCH

"And now to God the Father," he ends,
And his voice thrills up to the topmost tiles:
Each listener chokes as he bows and bends,
And emotion pervades the crowded aisles.
5 Then the preacher glides to the vestry-door,
And shuts it, and thinks he is seen no more.

The door swings softly ajar meanwhile,
And a pupil of his in the Bible class,
Who adores him as one without gloss or guile,
10 Sees her idol stand with a satisfied smile
And re-enact at the vestry-glass
Each pulpit gesture in deft dumb-show
That had moved the congregation so.

## III. By Her Aunt's Grave

"Sixpence a week," says the girl to her lover,
"Aunt used to bring me, for she could confide
In me alone, she vowed. 'Twas to cover
The cost of her headstone when she died.
5 And that was a year ago last June;
I've not yet fixed it. But I must soon."

"And where is the money now, my dear?"
"O, snug in my purse . . . Aunt was *so* slow
In saving it—eighty weeks, or near." . . .
10 "Let's spend it," he hints. "For she won't know
There's a dance to-night at the Load of Hay."
She passively nods. And they go that way.


## IV. In the Room of the Bride-Elect

"Would it had been the man of our wish!"
Sighs her mother. To whom with vehemence she
In the wedding-dress—the wife to be—
"Then why were you so mollyish
5 As not to insist on him for me!"
The mother, amazed: "Why, dearest one,
Because you pleaded for this or none!"

"But Father and you should have stood out strong!
Since then, to my cost, I have lived to find
10 That you were right and that I was wrong;
This man is a dolt to the one declined. . . .
Ah!—here he comes with his button-hole rose.
Good God—I must marry him I suppose!"

## V. At a Watering-Place

They sit and smoke on the esplanade,
The man and his friend, and regard the bay
Where the far chalk cliffs, to the left displayed,
Smile sallowly in the decline of day.
5  And saunterers pass with laugh and jest—
A handsome couple among the rest.

"That smart proud pair," says the man to his friend,
"Are to marry next week. . . . How little he thinks
That dozens of days and nights on end
10  I have stroked her neck, unhooked the links
Of her sleeve to get at her upper arm. . . .
Well, bliss is in ignorance: what's the harm!"

## VI. In the Cemetery

"You see those mothers squabbling there?"
Remarks the man of the cemetery.
"One says in tears, ' 'Tis mine lies here!'
Another, 'Nay, mine, you Pharisee!'
5  Another, 'How dare you move my flowers
And put your own on this grave of ours!'
But all their children were laid therein
At different times, like sprats in a tin.

"And then the main drain had to cross,
10  And we moved the lot some nights ago,
And packed them away in the general foss
With hundreds more. But their folks don't know,
And as well cry over a new-laid drain
As anything else, to ease your pain!"

## VII. Outside the Window

"My stick!" he says, and turns in the lane
To the house just left, whence a vixen voice
Comes out with the firelight through the pane,
And he sees within that the girl of his choice
Stands rating her mother with eyes aglare
For something said while he was there.

"At last I behold her soul undraped!"
Thinks the man who had loved her more than himself;
"My God!—'tis but narrowly I have escaped.—
My precious porcelain proves it delf."
His face has reddened like one ashamed,
And he steals off, leaving his stick unclaimed.

## VIII. In the Study

He enters, and mute on the edge of a chair
Sits a thin-faced lady, a stranger there,
A type of decayed gentility;
And by some small signs he well can guess
That she comes to him almost breakfastless.

"I have called—I hope I do not err—
I am looking for a purchaser
Of some score volumes of the works
Of eminent divines I own,—
Left by my father—though it irks
My patience to offer them." And she smiles
As if necessity were unknown;

"But the truth of it is that oftenwhiles
I have wished, as I am fond of art,
15    To make my rooms a little smart,
And these old books are so in the way."
And lightly still she laughs to him,
As if to sell were a mere gay whim,
And that, to be frank, Life were indeed
20    To her not vinegar and gall,
But fresh and honey-like; and Need
No household skeleton at all.


IX. At the Altar-Rail

"My bride is not coming, alas!" says the groom,
And the telegram shakes in his hand. "I own
It was hurried! We met at a dancing-room
When I went to the Cattle-Show alone,
5    And then, next night, where the Fountain leaps,
And the Street of the Quarter-Circle sweeps.

"Ay, she won me to ask her to be my wife—
'Twas foolish perhaps!—to forsake the ways
Of the flaring town for a farmer's life.
10    She agreed. And we fixed it. Now she says:
'It's sweet of you, dear, to prepare me a nest,
But a swift, short, gay life suits me best.
What I really am you have never gleaned;
I had eaten the apple ere you were weaned.' "

## X. In the Nuptial Chamber

"O that mastering tune!" And up in the bed
Like a lace-robed phantom springs the bride;
"And why?" asks the man she had that day wed,
With a start, as the band plays on outside.
"It's the townsfolk's cheery compliment
Because of our marriage, my Innocent."

"O but you don't know! 'Tis the passionate air
To which my old Love waltzed with me,
And I swore as we spun that none should share
My home, my kisses, till death, save he!
And he dominates me and thrills me through,
And it's he I embrace while embracing you!"

## XI. In the Restaurant

"But hear. If you stay, and the child be born,
It will pass as your husband's with the rest,
While, if we fly, the teeth of scorn
Will be gleaming at us from east to west;
And the child will come as a life despised;
I feel an elopement is ill-advised!"

"O you realize not what it is, my dear,
To a woman! Daily and hourly alarms
Lest the truth should out. How can I stay here,
And nightly take him into my arms!
Come to the child no name or fame,
Let us go, and face it, and bear the shame."

## XII. At the Draper's

"I stood at the back of the shop, my dear,
    But you did not perceive me.
Well, when they deliver what you were shown
    *I* shall know nothing of it, believe me!"

5  And he coughed and coughed as she paled and said,
    "O, I didn't see you come in there—
Why couldn't you speak?"—"Well, I didn't. I left
    That you should not notice I'd been there.

"You were viewing some lovely things. *'Soon required*
10    *For a widow, of latest fashion';*
And I knew 'twould upset you to meet the man
    Who had to be cold and ashen

"And screwed in a box before they could dress you
    *'In the last new note in mourning,'*
15  As they defined it. So, not to distress you,
    I left you to your adorning."

## XIII. On the Death-Bed

"I'll tell—being past all praying for—
Then promptly die. . . . He was out at the war,
And got some scent of the intimacy
That was under way between her and me;
5  And he stole back home, and appeared like a ghost
One night, at the very time almost
That I reached her house. Well, I shot him dead,
And secretly buried him. Nothing was said.

"The news of the battle came next day;
10  He was scheduled missing. I hurried away,
    Got out there, visited the field,
    And sent home word that a search revealed
    He was one of the slain; though, lying alone
    And stript, his body had not been known.

15  "But she suspected. I lost her love,
    Yea, my hope of earth, and of Heaven above;
    And my time's now come, and I'll pay the score,
    Though it be burning for evermore."


XIV. Over the Coffin

    They stand confronting, the coffin between,
    His wife of old, and his wife of late,
    And the dead man whose they both had been
    Seems listening aloof, as to things past date.
5   —"I have called," says the first. "Do you marvel or not?"
    "In truth," says the second, "I do—somewhat."

    "Well, there was a word to be said by me! . . .
    I divorced that man because of you—
    It seemed I must do it, boundenly;
10  But now I am older, and tell you true,
    For life is little, and dead lies he;
    I would I had let alone you two!
    And both of us, scorning parochial ways,
    Had lived like the wives in the patriarchs' days."

## XV. In the Moonlight

"O lonely workman, standing there
In a dream, why do you stare and stare
At her grave, as no other grave there were?

"If your great gaunt eyes so importune
5  Her soul by the shine of this corpse-cold moon
Maybe you'll raise her phantom soon!"

"Why, fool, it is what I would rather see
Than all the living folk there be;
But alas, there is no such joy for me!"

10  "Ah—she was one you loved, no doubt,
Through good and evil, through rain and drought,
And when she passed, all your sun went out?"

"Nay: she was the woman I did not love,
Whom all the others were ranked above,
15  Whom during her life I thought nothing of."

From
MOMENTS OF VISION
AND MISCELLANEOUS
VERSES

## "WE SAT AT THE WINDOW"
*(Bournemouth, 1875)*

We sat at the window looking out,
And the rain came down like silken strings
That Swithin's day. Each gutter and spout
Babbled unchecked in the busy way
5    Of witless things:
Nothing to read, nothing to see
Seemed in that room for her and me
    On Swithin's day.

We were irked by the scene, by our own selves; yes,
10  For I did not know, nor did she infer
How much there was to read and guess
By her in me, and to see and crown
    By me in her.
Wasted were two souls in their prime,
15  And great was the waste, that July time
    When the rain came down.


## AFTERNOON SERVICE AT MELLSTOCK

*(Circa 1850)*

On afternoons of drowsy calm
    We stood in the panelled pew,
Singing one-voiced a Tate-and-Brady psalm
    To the tune of "Cambridge New."

We watched the elms, we watched the rooks,
    The clouds upon the breeze,
Between the whiles of glancing at our books,
    And swaying like the trees.

So mindless were those outpourings!—
    Though I am not aware
That I have gained by subtle thought on things
    Since we stood psalming there.


## AT THE WORD "FAREWELL"

She looked like a bird from a cloud
    On the clammy lawn,
Moving alone, bare-browed
    In the dim of dawn.
The candles alight in the room
    For my parting meal
Made all things withoutdoors loom
    Strange, ghostly, unreal.


The hour itself was a ghost,
    And it seemed to me then
As of chances the chance furthermost
    I should see her again.
I beheld not where all was so fleet
    That a Plan of the past
Which had ruled us from birthtime to meet
    Was in working at last:


No prelude did I there perceive
    To a drama at all,
Or foreshadow what fortune might weave
    From beginnings so small;
But I rose as if quicked by a spur
    I was bound to obey,
And stepped through the casement to her
    Still alone in the gray.

"I am leaving you. . . . Farewell!" I said,
　　　As I followed her on
By an alley bare boughs overspread;
　　　"I soon must be gone!"
Even then the scale might have been turned
　　　Against love by a feather,
—But crimson one cheek of hers burned
　　　When we came in together.


## HEREDITY

I am the family face;
Flesh perishes, I live on,
Projecting trait and trace
Through time to times anon,
And leaping from place to place
Over oblivion.

The years-heired feature that can
In curve and voice and eye
Despise the human span
Of durance—that is I;
The eternal thing in man,
That heeds no call to die.


## NEAR LANIVET, 1872

There was a stunted handpost just on the crest,
　　　Only a few feet high:
She was tired, and we stopped in the twilight-time for her
　　　　　　　　　　　　　　　　rest,
　　　At the crossways close thereby.

She leant back, being so weary, against its stem,
　　And laid her arms on its own,
Each open palm stretched out to each end of them,
　　Her sad face sideways thrown.

Her white-clothed form at this dim-lit cease of day
　　Made her look as one crucified
In my gaze at her from the midst of the dusty way,
　　And hurriedly "Don't," I cried.

I do not think she heard. Loosing thence she said,
　　As she stepped forth ready to go,
"I am rested now.—Something strange came into my head;
　　I wish I had not leant so!"

And wordless we moved onward down from the hill
　　In the west cloud's murked obscure,
And looking back we could see the handpost still
　　In the solitude of the moor.

"It struck her too," I thought, for as if afraid
　　She heavily breathed as we trailed;
Till she said, "I did not think how 'twould look in the shade,
　　When I leant there like one nailed."

I, lightly: "There's nothing in it. For *you*, anyhow!"
　　—"O I know there is not," said she . . .
"Yet I wonder . . . If no one is bodily crucified now,
　　In spirit one may be!"

And we dragged on and on, while we seemed to see
　　In the running of Time's far glass
Her crucified, as she had wondered if she might be
　　Some day.—Alas, alas!

## To the Moon

"What have you looked at, Moon,
    In your time,
  Now long past your prime?"
"O, I have looked at, often looked at
5     Sweet, sublime,
Sore things, shudderful, night and noon
    In my time."

"What have you mused on, Moon,
    In your day,
10   So aloof, so far away?"
"O, I have mused on, often mused on
    Growth, decay,
Nations alive, dead, mad, aswoon,
    In my day!"

15  "Have you much wondered, Moon,
    On your rounds,
  Self-wrapt, beyond Earth's bounds?"
"Yea, I have wondered, often wondered
    At the sounds
20 Reaching me of the human tune
    On my rounds."

"What do you think of it, Moon,
    As you go?
  Is Life much, or no?"
25 "O, I think of it, often think of it
    As a show
God ought surely to shut up soon,
    As I go."

## TIMING HER
*(Written to an old folk-tune)*

Lalage's coming:
Where is she now, O?
Turning to bow, O,
And smile, is she,
5  Just at parting,
Parting, parting,
As she is starting
To come to me?

Where is she now, O,
10  Now, and now, O,
Shadowing a bough, O,
Of hedge or tree
As she is rushing,
Rushing, rushing,
15  Gossamers brushing
To come to me?

Lalage's coming;
Where is she now, O;
Climbing the brow, O,
20  Of hills I see?
Yes, she is nearing,
Nearing, nearing,
Weather unfearing
To come to me.

Near is she now, O,
Now, and now, O;
Milk the rich cow, O,
Forward the tea;
Shake the down bed for her,
Linen sheets spread for her,
Drape round the head for her
Coming to me.

Lalage's coming,
She's nearer now, O,
End anyhow, O,
To-day's husbandry!
Would a gilt chair were mine,
Slippers of vair were mine,
Brushes for hair were mine
Of ivory!

What will she think, O,
She who's so comely,
Viewing how homely
A sort we are!
Nothing resplendent,
No prompt attendant,
Not one dependent
Pertaining to me!

Lalage's coming;
Where is she now, O?
Fain I'd avow, O,
Full honestly
Nought here's enough for her,
All is too rough for her,
Even my love for her
Poor in degree.

She's nearer now, O,
Still nearer now, O,
She 'tis, I vow, O,
60  Passing the lea.
Rush down to meet her there,
Call out and greet her there,
Never a sweeter there
Crossed to me!

65  Lalage's come; aye,
Come is she now, O! . . .
Does Heaven allow, O,
A meeting to be?
Yes, she is here now,
70  Here now, here now,
Nothing to fear now,
Here's Lalage!


## THE BLINDED BIRD

So zestfully canst thou sing?
And all this indignity,
With God's consent, on thee!
Blinded ere yet a-wing
5  By the red-hot needle thou,
I stand and wonder how
So zestfully thou canst sing!

Resenting not such wrong,
Thy grievous pain forgot,
10  Eternal dark thy lot,
Groping thy whole life long,
After that stab of fire;
Enjailed in pitiless wire;
Resenting not such wrong!

5  Who hath charity? This bird.
   Who suffereth long and is kind,
   Is not provoked, though blind
   And alive ensepulchred?
   Who hopeth, endureth all things?
10 Who thinketh no evil, but sings?
   Who is divine? This bird.


## "THE WIND BLEW WORDS"

The wind blew words along the skies,
    And these it blew to me
Through the wide dusk: "Lift up your eyes,
    Behold this troubled tree,
5  Complaining as it sways and plies;
    It is a limb of thee.

"Yea, too, the creatures sheltering round—
    Dumb figures, wild and tame,
Yea, too, thy fellows who abound—
    Either of speech the same
Or far and strange—black, dwarfed, and browned,
    They are stuff of thy own frame."

I moved on in a surging awe
    Of inarticulateness
At the pathetic Me I saw
    In all his huge distress,
Making self-slaughter of the law
    To kill, break, or suppress.

## To My Father's Violin

Does he want you down there
In the Nether Glooms where
The hours may be a dragging load upon him,
As he hears the axle grind
Round and round
Of the great world, in the blind
Still profound
Of the night-time? He might liven at the sound
Of your string, revealing you had not forgone him.

In the gallery west the nave,
But a few yards from his grave,
Did you, tucked beneath his chin, to his bowing
Guide the homely harmony
Of the quire
Who for long years strenuously—
Son and sire—
Caught the strains that at his fingering low or higher
From your four thin threads and eff-holes came outflowing.

And, too, what merry tunes
He would bow at nights or noons
That chanced to find him bent to lute a measure,
When he made you speak his heart
As in dream,
Without book or music-chart,
On some theme
Elusive as a jack-o'-lanthorn's gleam,
And the psalm of duty shelved for trill of pleasure.

Well, you can not, alas,
    The barrier overpass
That screens him in those Mournful Meads hereunder,
    Where no fiddling can be heard
        In the glades
    Of silentness, no bird
        Thrills the shades;
Where no viol is touched for songs or serenades,
No bowing wakes a congregation's wonder.

    He must do without you now,
    Stir you no more anyhow
To yearning concords taught you in your glory;
    While, your strings a tangled wreck,
        Once smart drawn,
    Ten worm-wounds in your neck,
        Purflings wan
With dust-hoar, here alone I sadly con
Your present dumbness, shape your olden story.

## THE PEDIGREE

### I

    I bent in the deep of night
    Over a pedigree the chronicler gave
    As mine; and as I bent there, half-unrobed,
The uncurtained panes of my window-square let in the
                          watery light
    Of the moon in its old age:
And green-rheumed clouds were hurrying past where mute
                         and cold it globed
    Like a drifting dolphin's eye seen through a lapping wave.

## II

So, scanning my sire-sown tree,
And the hieroglyphs of this spouse tied to that,
10      With offspring mapped below in lineage,
Till the tangles troubled me,
The branches seemed to twist into a seared and cynic face
Which winked and tokened towards the window like a
                                                    Mage
Enchanting me to gaze again thereat.


## III

15      It was a mirror now,
And in it a long perspective I could trace
Of my begetters, dwindling backward each past each
All with the kindred look,
Whose names had since been inked down in their place
20      On the recorder's book,
Generation and generation of my mien, and build, and brow.


## IV

And then did I divine
That every heave and coil and move I made
Within my brain, and in my mood and speech,
25      Was in the glass portrayed
As long forestalled by their so making it,
The first of them, the primest fuglemen of my line,
Being fogged in far antiqueness past surmise and reason's
                                                    reach.

Said I then, sunk in tone,
"I am merest mimicker and counterfeit!—
Though thinking, *I am I,
And what I do I do myself alone.*"
—The cynic twist of the page thereat unknit
Back to its normal figure, having wrought its purport wry,
The Mage's mirror left the window-square,
And the stained moon and drift retook their places there.


## WHERE THEY LIVED

Dishevelled leaves creep down
Upon that bank to-day,
Some green, some yellow, and some pale brown;
The wet bents bob and sway;
The once warm slippery turf is sodden
Where we laughingly sat or lay.

The summerhouse is gone,
Leaving a weedy space;
The bushes that veiled it once have grown
Gaunt trees that interlace,
Through whose lank limbs I see too clearly
The nakedness of the place.

And where were hills of blue,
Blind drifts of vapour blow,
And the names of former dwellers few,
If any, people know,
And instead of a voice that called, "Come in, Dears,"
Time calls, "Pass below!"

## "SOMETHING TAPPED"

Something tapped on the pane of my room
    When there was never a trace
Of wind or rain, and I saw in the gloom
    My weary Belovéd's face.

5  "O I am tired of waiting," she said,
    "Night, morn, noon, afternoon;
So cold it is in my lonely bed,
    And I thought you would join me soon!"

I rose and neared the window-glass,
10    But vanished thence had she:
Only a pallid moth, alas,
    Tapped at the pane for me.

*August 1913*

## THE OXEN

Christmas Eve, and twelve of the clock.
    "Now they are all on their knees,"
An elder said as we sat in a flock
    By the embers in hearthside ease.

5  We pictured the meek mild creatures where
    They dwelt in their strawy pen,
Nor did it occur to one of us there
    To doubt they were kneeling then.

So fair a fancy few would weave
In these years! Yet, I feel,
If someone said on Christmas Eve,
"Come; see the oxen kneel

"In the lonely barton by yonder coomb
Our childhood used to know,"
I should go with him in the gloom,
Hoping it might be so.


## THE PHOTOGRAPH

The flame crept up the portrait line by line
As it lay on the coals in the silence of night's profound,
And over the arm's incline,
And along the marge of the silkwork superfine,
And gnawed at the delicate bosom's defenceless round.

Then I vented a cry of hurt, and averted my eyes;
The spectacle was one that I could not bear,
To my deep and sad surprise;
But, compelled to heed, I again looked furtivewise
Till the flame had eaten her breasts, and mouth, and hair.

"Thank God, she is out of it now!" I said at last,
In a great relief of heart when the thing was done
That had set my soul aghast,
And nothing was left of the picture unsheathed from the past
But the ashen ghost of the card it had figured on.

She was a woman long hid amid packs of years,
She might have been living or dead; she was lost to my sight,
And the deed that had nigh drawn tears
Was done in a casual clearance of life's arrears;
But I felt as if I had put her to death that night! . . .

—Well; she knew nothing thereof did she survive,
And suffered nothing if numbered among the dead;
  Yet—yet—if on earth alive
Did she feel a smart, and with vague strange anguish strive?
25 If in heaven, did she smile at me sadly and shake her head?


## AN ANNIVERSARY

It was at the very date to which we have come,
 In the month of the matching name,
When, at a like minute, the sun had upswum,
 Its couch-time at night being the same.
5 And the same path stretched here that people now follow,
 And the same stile crossed their way,
And beyond the same green hillock and hollow
 The same horizon lay;
And the same man pilgrims now hereby who pilgrimed here
       that day.


10 Let so much be said of the date-day's sameness;
 But the tree that neighbours the track,
And stoops liked a pedlar afflicted with lameness,
 Knew of no sogged wound or wind-crack.
And the joints of that wall were not enshrouded
15 With mosses of many tones,
And the garth up afar was not overcrowded
 With a multitude of white stones,
And the man's eyes then were not so sunk that you saw the
       socket-bones.

## TRANSFORMATIONS

Portion of this yew
Is a man my grandsire knew,
Bosomed here at its foot:
This branch may be his wife,
A ruddy human life
Now turned to a green shoot.

These grasses must be made
Of her who often prayed,
Last century, for repose;
And the fair girl long ago
Whom I vainly tried to know
May be entering this rose.

So, they are not underground,
But as nerves and veins abound
In the growths of upper air,
And they feel the sun and rain,
And the energy again
That made them what they were!


## THE LAST SIGNAL
*A Memory of William Barnes*

*(11 October 1886)*

Silently I footed by an uphill road
That led from my abode to a spot yew-boughed;
Yellowly the sun sloped low down to westward,
And dark was the east with cloud.

Then, amid the shadow of that livid sad east,
    Where the light was least, and a gate stood wide,
Something flashed the fire of the sun that was facing it,
        Like a brief blaze on that side.

Looking hard and harder I knew what it meant—
    The sudden shine sent from the livid east scene;
It meant the west mirrored by the coffin of my friend there,
        Turning to the road from his green,

To take his last journey forth—he who in his prime
    Trudged so many a time from that gate athwart the land!
Thus a farewell to me he signalled on his grave-way,
        As with a wave of his hand.

*Winterborne-Came Path*

## GREAT THINGS

Sweet cyder is a great thing,
    A great thing to me,
Spinning down to Weymouth town
    By Ridgway thirstily,
And maid and mistress summoning
    Who tend the hostelry:
O cyder is a great thing,
    A great thing to me!

The dance it is a great thing,
    A great thing to me,
With candles lit and partners fit
    For night-long revelry;
And going home when day-dawning
    Peeps pale upon the lea:
O dancing is a great thing,
    A great thing to me!

Love is, yea, a great thing,
    A great thing to me,
When, having drawn across the lawn
20    In darkness silently,
A figure flits like one a-wing
    Out from the nearest tree:
O love is, yes, a great thing,
    A great thing to me!


25 Will these be always great things,
    Great things to me? . . .
Let it befall that One will call,
    "Soul, I have need of thee":
What then? Joy-jaunts, impassioned flings,
30    Love, and its ecstasy,
Will always have been great things,
    Great things to me!


## At Middle-Field Gate in February

The bars are thick with drops that show
    As they gather themselves from the fog
Like silver buttons ranged in a row,
And as evenly spaced as if measured, although
5    They fall at the feeblest jog.


They load the leafless hedge hard by,
    And the blades of last year's grass,
While the fallow ploughland turned up nigh
In raw rolls clammy and clogging lie—
10    Too clogging for feet to pass.

How dry it was on a far-back day
    When straws hung the hedge and around,
When amid the sheaves in amorous play
In curtained bonnets and light array
15    Bloomed a bevy now underground!

*Bockhampton Lane*


## On Sturminster Foot-Bridge

Reticulations creep upon the slack stream's face
    When the wind skims irritably past,
The current clucks smartly into each hollow place
That years of flood have scrabbled in the pier's sodden base;
5    The floating-lily leaves rot fast.

On a roof stand the swallows ranged in wistful waiting rows,
    Till they arrow off and drop like stones
Among the eyot-withies at whose foot the river flows:
And beneath the roof is she who in the dark world shows
10    As a lattice-gleam when midnight moans.


## Old Furniture

I know not how it may be with others
    Who sit amid relics of householdry
That date from the days of their mothers' mothers,
    But well I know how it is with me
5      Continually.

I see the hands of the generations
　　That owned each shiny familiar thing
In play on its knobs and indentations,
　　And with its ancient fashioning
10　　　Still dallying:

Hands behind hands, growing paler and paler,
　　As in a mirror a candle-flame
Shows images of itself, each frailer
　　As it recedes, though the eye may frame
15　　　Its shape the same.

On the clock's dull dial a foggy finger,
　　Moving to set the minutes right
With tentative touches that lift and linger
　　In the wont of a moth on a summer night,
20　　　Creeps to my sight.

On this old viol, too, fingers are dancing—
　　As whilom—just over the strings by the nut,
The tip of a bow receding, advancing
　　In airy quivers, as if it would cut
25　　　The plaintive gut.

And I see a face by that box for tinder,
　　Glowing forth in fits from the dark,
And fading again, as the linten cinder
　　Kindles to red at the flinty spark,
30　　　Or goes out stark.

Well, well. It is best to be up and doing,
　　The world has no use for one to-day
Who eyes things thus—no aim pursuing!
　　He should not continue in this stay,
35　　　But sink away.

## A THOUGHT IN TWO MOODS

I saw it—pink and white—revealed
    Upon the white and green;
The white and green was a daisied field,
    The pink and white Ethleen.

5  And as I looked it seemed in kind
    That difference they had none;
The two fair bodiments combined
    As varied miens of one.

A sense that, in some mouldering year,
10    As one they both would lie,
Made me move quickly on to her
    To pass the pale thought by.

She laughed and said: "Out there, to me,
    You looked so weather-browned,
15 And brown in clothes, you seemed to be
    Made of the dusty ground!"


## LOGS ON THE HEARTH
*A Memory of a Sister*

The fire advances along the log
    Of the tree we felled,
Which bloomed and bore striped apples by the peck
    Till its last hour of bearing knelled.

5    The fork that first my hand would reach
      And then my foot,
In climbings upward inch by inch, lies now
    Sawn, sapless, darkening with soot.

Where the bark chars is where, one year,
     It was pruned, and bled—
Then overgrew the wound. But now, at last,
    Its growings all have stagnated.

My fellow-climber rises dim
     From her chilly grave—
Just as she was, her foot near mine on the bending limb,
    Laughing, her young brown hand awave.

*December 1915*


## THE CAGED GOLDFINCH

Within a churchyard, on a recent grave,
    I saw a little cage
That jailed a goldfinch. All was silence save
    Its hops from stage to stage.

There was inquiry in its wistful eye,
    And once it tried to sing;
Of him or her who placed it there, and why,
    No one knew anything.


## THE BALLET

They crush together—a rustling heap of flesh—
Of more than flesh, a heap of souls; and then
    They part, enmesh,
    And crush together again,
Like the pink petals of a too sanguine rose
    Frightened shut just when it blows.

Though all alike in their tinsel livery,
And indistinguishable at a sweeping glance,
      They muster, maybe,
10        As lives wide in irrelevance;
A world of her own has each one underneath,
      Detached as a sword from its sheath.

Daughters, wives, mistresses; honest or false, sold, bought;
Hearts of all sizes; gay, fond, gushing, or penned,
15        Various in thought
      Of lover, rival, friend;
Links in a one-pulsed chain, all showing one smile,
      Yet severed so many a mile!


## THE FIVE STUDENTS

      The sparrow dips in his wheel-rut bath,
        The sun grows passionate-eyed,
    And boils the dew to smoke by the paddock-path;
        As strenuously we stride,—
5  Five of us; dark He, fair He, dark She, fair She, I,
         All beating by.

      The air is shaken, the high-road hot,
        Shadowless swoons the day,
    The greens are sobered and cattle at rest; but not
10        We on our urgent way,—
Four of us; fair She, dark She, fair He, I, are there,
        But one—elsewhere.

      Autumn moulds the hard fruit mellow,
        And forward still we press
15      Through moors, briar-meshed plantations,
                  clay-pits yellow,
        As in the spring hours—yes,
Three of us; fair He, fair She, I, as heretofore,
        But—fallen one more.

The leaf drops: earthworms draw it in
        At night-time noiselessly,
    The fingers of birch and beech are skeleton-thin,
        And yet on the beat are we,—
Two of us; fair She, I. But no more left to go
        The track we know.


        Icicles tag the church-aisle leads,
            The flag-rope gibbers hoarse,
        The home-bound foot-folk wrap their snow-flaked heads,
            Yet I still stalk the course,—
    One of us. . . . Dark and fair He, dark and fair She, gone:
            The rest—anon.


## During Wind and Rain

        They sing their dearest songs—
        He, she, all of them—yea,
        Treble and tenor and bass,
            And one to play;
        With the candles mooning each face. . . .
            Ah, no; the years O!
    How the sick leaves reel down in throngs!


        They clear the creeping moss—
        Elders and juniors—aye,
        Making the pathways neat
            And the garden gay;
        And they build a shady seat. . . .
            Ah, no; the years, the years;
    See, the white storm-birds wing across.

They are blithely breakfasting all—
        Men and maidens—yea,
        Under the summer tree,
            With a glimpse of the bay,
        While pet fowl come to the knee. . . .
Ah, no; the years O!
And the rotten rose is ript from the wall.

        They change to a high new house,
        He, she, all of them—aye,
        Clocks and carpets and chairs
On the lawn all day,
        And brightest things that are theirs. . . .
            Ah, no; the years, the years;
Down their carved names the rain-drop ploughs.


## HE PREFERS HER EARTHLY

This after-sunset is a sight for seeing,
Cliff-heads of craggy cloud surrounding it.
    —And dwell you in that glory-show?
You may; for there are strange strange things in being,
Stranger than I know.

Yet if that chasm of splendour claim your presence
Which glows between the ash cloud and the dun,
    How changed must be your mortal mould!
Changed to a firmament-riding earthless essence
From what you were of old:

All too unlike the fond and fragile creature
Then known to me. . . . Well, shall I say it plain?
    I would not have you thus and there,
But still would grieve on, missing you, still feature
You as the one you were.


132

## A BACKWARD SPRING

The trees are afraid to put forth buds,
And there is timidity in the grass;
The plots lie gray where gouged by spuds,
    And whether next week will pass
5 Free of sly sour winds is the fret of each bush
      Of barberry waiting to bloom.

Yet the snowdrop's face betrays no gloom,
And the primrose pants in its heedless push,
Though the myrtle asks if it's worth the fight
10     This year with frost and rime
      To venture one more time
On delicate leaves and buttons of white
From the selfsame bough as at last year's prime,
And never to ruminate on or remember
15 What happened to it in mid-December.


## "WHO'S IN THE NEXT ROOM?"

   "Who's in the next room?—who?
      I seemed to see
Somebody in the dawning passing through,
     Unknown to me."
5 "Nay: you saw nought. He passed invisibly."

   "Who's in the next room?—who?
      I seem to hear
Somebody muttering firm in a language new
     That chills the ear."
0 "No: you catch not his tongue who has entered there."

"Who's in the next room?—who?
　　　I seem to feel
His breath like a clammy draught, as if it drew
　　　From the Polar Wheel."
15　"No: none who breathes at all does the door conceal."

"Who's in the next room?—who?
　　　A figure wan
With a message to one in there of something due?
　　　Shall I know him anon?"
20　"Yea he; and he brought such; and you'll know him anon."


## AT A COUNTRY FAIR

At a bygone Western country fair
I saw a giant led by a dwarf
With a red string like a long thin scarf;
How much he was the stronger there
5　　　The giant seemed unaware.

And then I saw that the giant was blind,
And the dwarf a shrewd-eyed little thing;
The giant, mild, timid, obeyed the string
As if he had no independent mind,
10　　　Or will of any kind.

Wherever the dwarf decided to go
At his heels the other trotted meekly,
(Perhaps—I know not—reproaching weakly)
Like one Fate bade that it must be so,
15　　　Whether he wished or no.

Various sights in various climes
I have seen, and more I may see yet,
But that sight never shall I forget,
And have thought it the sorriest of pantomimes,
20　　　If once, a hundred times!

# JUBILATE

"The very last time I ever was here," he said,
"I saw much less of the quick than I saw of the dead."
—He was a man I had met with somewhere before,
But how or when I now could recall no more.

"The hazy mazy moonlight at one in the morning
Spread out as a sea across the frozen snow,
Glazed to live sparkles like the great breastplate adorning
The priest of the Temple, with Urim and Thummim aglow.

"The yew-tree arms, glued hard to the stiff stark air,
Hung still in the village sky as theatre-scenes
When I came by the churchyard wall, and halted there
At a shut-in sound of fiddles and tambourines.

"And as I stood hearkening, dulcimers, hautboys, and
                                        shawms,
And violoncellos, and a three-stringed double-bass,
Joined in, and were intermixed with a singing of psalms;
And I looked over at the dead men's dwelling-place.

"Through the shine of the slippery snow I now could see,
As it were through a crystal roof, a great company
Of the dead minueting in stately step underground
To the tune of the instruments I had before heard sound.

"It was 'Eden New,' and dancing they sang in a chore,
'We are out of it all!—yea, in Little-Ease cramped no
                                        more!'
And their shrouded figures pacing with joy I could see
As you see the stage from the gallery. And they had no heed
                                        of me.

25 "And I lifted my head quite dazed from the churchyard wall
And I doubted not that it warned I should soon have my
call.
But—" . . . Then in the ashes he emptied the dregs of his
cup,
And onward he went, and the darkness swallowed him up.


## Midnight on the Great Western

In the third-class seat sat the journeying boy,
    And the roof-lamp's oily flame
Played down on his listless form and face,
Bewrapt past knowing to what he was going,
5     Or whence he came.

In the band of his hat the journeying boy
    Had a ticket stuck; and a string
Around his neck bore the key of his box,
That twinkled gleams of the lamp's sad beams
10     Like a living thing.

What past can be yours, O journeying boy
    Towards a world unknown,
Who calmly, as if incurious quite
On all at stake, can undertake
15     This plunge alone?

Knows your soul a sphere, O journeying boy,
    Our rude realms far above,
Whence with spacious vision you mark and mete
This region of sin that you find you in,
20     But are not of?

## THE SHADOW ON THE STONE

    I went by the Druid stone
  That broods in the garden white and lone,
And I stopped and looked at the shifting shadows
    That at some moments fall thereon
5    From the tree hard by with a rhythmic swing,
    And they shaped in my imagining
To the shade that a well-known head and shoulders
    Threw there when she was gardening.

    I thought her behind my back,
10    Yea, her I long had learned to lack,
And I said: "I am sure you are standing behind me,
    Though how do you get into this old track?"
    And there was no sound but the fall of a leaf
    As a sad response; and to keep down grief
15 I would not turn my head to discover
    That there was nothing in my belief.

    Yet I wanted to look and see
    That nobody stood at the back of me;
But I thought once more: "Nay, I'll not unvision
20    A shape which, somehow, there may be."
    So I went on softly from the glade,
    And left her behind me throwing her shade,
As she were indeed an apparition—
    My head unturned lest my dream should fade.

## IN THE GARDEN
*(M.H.)*

We waited for the sun
To break its cloudy prison
(For day was not yet done,
And night still unbegun)
5  Leaning by the dial.

After many a trial—
We all silent there—
It burst as new-arisen,
Shading its finger where
10  Time travelled at that minute.

Little saw we in it,
But this much I know,
Of lookers on that shade,
Her towards whom it made
15  Soonest had to go.

*1915*


## AN UPBRAIDING

Now I am dead you sing to me
    The songs we used to know,
But while I lived you had no wish
    Or care for doing so.

5  Now I am dead you come to me
    In the moonlight, comfortless;
Ah, what would I have given alive
    To win such tenderness!

When you are dead, and stand to me
10      Not differenced, as now,
But like again, will you be cold
        As when we lived, or how?


## THE CHOIRMASTER'S BURIAL

He often would ask us
That, when he died,
After playing so many
To their last rest,
5   If out of us any
Should here abide,
And it would not task us,
We would with our lutes
Play over him
10  By his grave-brim
The psalm he liked best—
The one whose sense suits
"Mount Ephraim"—
And perhaps we should seem
15  To him, in Death's dream,
Like the seraphim.

As soon as I knew
That his spirit was gone
I thought this his due,
20  And spoke thereupon.

"I think," said the vicar,
"A read service quicker
Than viols out-of-doors
In these frosts and hoars.

25 That old-fashioned way
Requires a fine day,
And it seems to me
It had better not be."

Hence, that afternoon,
30 Though never knew he
That his wish could not be,
To get through it faster
They buried the master
Without any tune.

35 But 'twas said that, when
At the dead of next night
The vicar looked out,
There struck on his ken
Thronged roundabout,
40 Where the frost was graying
The headstoned grass,
A band all in white
Like the saints in church-glass,
Singing and playing
45 The ancient stave
By the choirmaster's grave.

Such the tenor man told
When he had grown old.

# In Time of "The Breaking of Nations"

## I

Only a man harrowing clods
   In a slow silent walk
With an old horse that stumbles and nods
   Half asleep as they stalk.

## II

5 Only thin smoke without flame
   From the heaps of couch-grass;
Yet this will go onward the same
   Though Dynasties pass.

## III

Yonder a maid and her wight
10    Come whispering by:
War's annals will cloud into night
   Ere their story die.

## AFTERWARDS

When the Present has latched its postern behind my
                         tremulous stay,
  And the May month flaps its glad green leaves like wings,
Delicate-filmed as new-spun silk, will the neighbours say,
  "He was a man who used to notice such things"?

5  If it be in the dusk when, like an eyelid's soundless blink,
  The dewfall-hawk comes crossing the shades to alight
Upon the wind-warped upland thorn, a gazer may think,
  "To him this must have been a familiar sight."

If I pass during some nocturnal blackness, mothy and warm,
10    When the hedgehog travels furtively over the lawn,
One may say, "He strove that such innocent creatures
                    should come to no harm,
  But he could do little for them; and now he is gone."

If, when hearing that I have been stilled at last, they
                    stand at the door,
  Watching the full-starred heavens that winter sees,
15  Will this thought rise on those who will meet my face no
                    more,
  "He was one who had an eye for such mysteries"?

And will any say when my bell of quittance is heard in
                    the gloom,
  And a crossing breeze cuts a pause in its outrollings,
Till they swell again, as they were a new bell's boom,
20    "He hears it not now, but used to notice such things"?

From
LATE LYRICS
AND EARLIER

## WEATHERS

### I

This is the weather the cuckoo likes,
    And so do I;
When showers betumble the chestnut spikes,
    And nestlings fly:
5  And the little brown nightingale bills his best,
And they sit outside at "The Travellers' Rest,"
And maids come forth sprig-muslin drest,
And citizens dream of the south and west,
    And so do I.

### II

10  This is the weather the shepherd shuns,
    And so do I;
When beeches drip in browns and duns,
    And thresh, and ply;
And hill-hid tides throb, throe on throe,
15  And meadow rivulets overflow,
And drops on gate-bars hang in a row,
And rooks in families homeward go,
    And so do I.

## THE GARDEN SEAT

Its former green is blue and thin,
And its once firm legs sink in and in;
Soon it will break down unaware,
Soon it will break down unaware.

5  At night when reddest flowers are black
   Those who once sat thereon come back;
   Quite a row of them sitting there,
   Quite a row of them sitting there.

   With them the seat does not break down,
10 Nor winter freeze them, nor floods drown,
   For they are as light as upper air,
   They are as light as upper air!


## "ACCORDING TO THE MIGHTY WORKING"

### I

When moiling seems at cease
      In the vague void of night-time,
      And heaven's wide roomage stormless
      Between the dusk and light-time,
5      And fear at last is formless,
We call the allurement Peace.


### II

Peace, this hid riot, Change,
      This revel of quick-cued mumming,
      This never truly being,
10      This evermore becoming,
      This spinner's wheel onfleeing
Outside perception's range.

                                        *1917*

## GOING AND STAYING

### I

The moving sun-shapes on the spray,
The sparkles where the brook was flowing,
Pink faces, plightings, moonlit May,
These were the things we wished would stay;
     But they were going.

### II

Seasons of blankness as of snow,
The silent bleed of a world decaying,
The moan of multitudes in woe,
These were the things we wished would go;
     But they were staying.

### III

Then we looked closelier at Time,
And saw his ghostly arms revolving
To sweep off woeful things with prime,
Things sinister with things sublime
     Alike dissolving.

## The Contretemps

A forward rush by the lamp in the gloom,
   And we clasped, and almost kissed;
But she was not the woman whom
I had promised to meet in the thawing brume
5  On that harbour-bridge; nor was I he of her tryst.

So loosening from me swift she said:
   "O why, why feign to be
The one I had meant!—to whom I have sped
To fly with, being so sorrily wed!"
10  —'Twas thus and thus that she upbraided me.

My assignation had struck upon
   Some others' like it, I found.
And her lover rose on the night anon;
And then her husband entered on
15  The lamplit, snowflaked, sloppiness around.

"Take her and welcome, man!" he cried:
   "I wash my hands of her.
I'll find me twice as good a bride!"
—All this to me, whom he had eyed,
20  'Twas clear, as his wife's planned deliverer.

And next the lover: "Little I knew,
   Madam, you had a third!
Kissing here in my very view!"
—Husband and lover then withdrew.
25  I let them; and I told them not they erred.

Why not? Well, there faced she and I—
   Two strangers who'd kissed, or near,
Chancewise. To see stand weeping by

A woman once embraced, will try
30    The tension of a man the most austere.

So it began; and I was young,
    She pretty, by the lamp,
As flakes came waltzing down among
The waves of her clinging hair, that hung
35    Heavily on her temples, dark and damp.

And there alone still stood we two;
    She one cast off for me,
Or so it seemed: while night ondrew,
Forcing a parley what should do
40    We twain hearts caught in one catastrophe.

In stranded souls a common strait
    Wakes latencies unknown,
Whose impulse may precipitate
A life-long leap. The hour was late,
45    And there was the Jersey boat with its funnel agroan.

"Is wary walking worth much pother?"
    It grunted, as still it stayed.
"One pairing is as good as another
Where all is venture! Take each other,
50    And scrap the oaths that you have aforetime made." . . .

—Of the four involved there walks but one
    On earth at this late day.
And what of the chapter so begun?
In that odd complex what was done?
55    Well; happiness comes in full to none:
Let peace lie on lulled lips: I will not say.

*Weymouth*

## A Night in November

I marked when the weather changed,
And the panes began to quake,
And the winds rose up and ranged,
That night, lying half-awake.

5 Dead leaves blew into my room,
And alighted upon my bed,
And a tree declared to the gloom
Its sorrow that they were shed.

One leaf of them touched my hand,
10 And I thought that it was you
There stood as you used to stand,
And saying at last you knew!

## The Fallow Deer at the Lonely House

One without looks in to-night
  Through the curtain-chink
From the sheet of glistening white;
One without looks in to-night
5   As we sit and think
  By the fender-brink.

We do not discern those eyes
  Watching in the snow;
Lit by lamps of rosy dyes
10 We do not discern those eyes
   Wondering, aglow,
   Fourfooted, tiptoe.

## ON THE TUNE CALLED
## THE OLD-HUNDRED-AND-FOURTH

We never sang together
   Ravenscroft's terse old tune
On Sundays or on weekdays,
In sharp or summer weather,
   At night-time or at noon.

Why did we never sing it,
   Why never so incline
On Sundays or on weekdays,
Even when soft wafts would wing it
   From your far floor to mine?

Shall we that tune, then, never
   Stand voicing side by side
On Sundays or on weekdays? . . .
Or shall we, when for ever
   In Sheol we abide,

Sing it in desolation,
   As we might long have done
On Sundays or on weekdays
With love and exultation
   Before our sands had run?

151

## Voices from Things Growing in a Churchyard

These flowers are I, poor Fanny Hurd,
      Sir or Madam,
A little girl here sepultured.
Once I flit-fluttered like a bird
Above the grass, as now I wave
In daisy shapes above my grave,
      All day cheerily,
      All night eerily!

—I am one Bachelor Bowring, "Gent,"
      Sir or Madam;
In shingled oak my bones were pent;
Hence more than a hundred years I spent
In my feat of change from a coffin-thrall
To a dancer in green as leaves on a wall,
      All day cheerily,
      All night eerily!

—I, these berries of juice and gloss,
      Sir or Madam,
Am clean forgotten as Thomas Voss;
Thin-urned, I have burrowed away from the moss
That covers my sod, and have entered this yew,
And turned to clusters ruddy of view,
      All day cheerily,
      All night eerily!

—The Lady Gertrude, proud, high-bred,
      Sir or Madam,
Am I—this laurel that shades your head;
Into its veins I have stilly sped,
And made them of me; and my leaves now shine,
As did my satins superfine,
      All day cheerily,
      All night eerily!

—I, who as innocent withwind climb,
      Sir or Madam,
35  Am one Eve Greensleeves, in olden time
Kissed by men from many a clime,
Beneath sun, stars, in blaze, in breeze,
As now by glowworms and by bees,
      All day cheerily,
40        All night eerily!

—I'm old Squire Audeley Grey, who grew,
      Sir or Madam,
Aweary of life, and in scorn withdrew;
Till anon I clambered up anew
45  As ivy-green, when my ache was stayed,
And in that attire I have longtime gayed
      All day cheerily,
      All night eerily!

—And so these maskers breathe to each
50      Sir or Madam
Who lingers there, and their lively speech
Affords an interpreter much to teach,
As their murmurous accents seem to come
Thence hitheraround in a radiant hum,
55      All day cheerily,
      All night eerily!

# A Two-Years' Idyll

        Yes; such it was;
      Just those two seasons unsought,
Sweeping like summertide wind on our ways;
        Moving, as straws,
5       Hearts quick as ours in those days;
Going like wind, too, and rated as nought
        Save as the prelude to plays
        Soon to come—larger, life-fraught:
          Yes; such it was.


10        "Nought" it was called,
        Even by ourselves—that which springs
Out of the years for all flesh, first or last,
        Commonplace, scrawled
        Dully on days that go past.
15   Yet, all the while, it upbore us like wings
        Even in hours overcast:
        Aye, though this best thing of things,
          "Nought" it was called!


        What seems it now?
20        Lost: such beginning was all;
Nothing came after: romance straight forsook
        Quickly somehow
        Life when we sped from our nook,
Primed for new scenes with designs smart and tall. . . .
25        —A preface without any book,
        A trumpet uplipped, but no call;
          That seems it now.

## FETCHING HER

An hour before the dawn,
    My friend,
You lit your waiting bedside-lamp,
    Your breakfast-fire anon,
And outing into the dark and damp
    You saddled, and set on.

Thuswise, before the day,
    My friend,
You sought her on her surfy shore,
    To fetch her thence away
Unto your own new-built door
    For a staunch lifelong stay.

You said: "It seems to be,
    My friend,
That I were bringing to my place
    The pure brine breeze, the sea,
The mews—all her old sky and space,
    In bringing her with me!"

—But time is prompt to expugn,
    My friend,
Such magic-minted conjurings:
    The brought breeze fainted soon,
And then the sense of seamews' wings,
    And the shore's sibilant tune.

So, it had been more due,
    My friend,
Perhaps, had you not pulled this flower
    From the craggy nook it knew,
And set it in an alien bower;
    But left it where it grew!

## A Procession of Dead Days

I see the ghost of a perished day;
I know his face, and the feel of his dawn:
'Twas he who took me far away
    To a spot strange and gray:
5  Look at me, Day, and then pass on,
But come again: yes, come anon!

Enters another into view;
His features are not cold or white,
But rosy as a vein seen through:
10    Too soon he smiles adieu.
Adieu, O ghost-day of delight;
But come and grace my dying sight.

Enters the day that brought the kiss:
He brought it in his foggy hand
15  To where the mumbling river is,
    And the high clematis;
It lent new colour to the land,
And all the boy within me manned.

Ah, this one. Yes, I know his name,
20  He is the day that wrought a shine
Even on a precinct common and tame,
    As 'twere of purposed aim.
He shows him as a rainbow sign
Of promise made to me and mine.

25  The next stands forth in his morning clothes,
And yet, despite their misty blue,
They mark no sombre custom-growths
    That joyous living loathes,
But a meteor act, that left in its queue
30  A train of sparks my lifetime through.

I almost tremble at his nod—
This next in train—who looks at me
As I were slave, and he were god
   Wielding an iron rod.
35  I close my eyes; yet still is he
In front there, looking mastery.

In semblance of a face averse
The phantom of the next one comes:
I did not know what better or worse
40    Chancings might bless or curse
When his original glossed the thrums
Of ivy, bringing that which numbs.

Yes; trees were turning in their sleep
Upon their windy pillows of gray
45  When he stole in. Silent his creep
    On the grassed eastern steep. . . .
I shall not soon forget that day,
And what his third hour took away!


## In the Small Hours

I lay in my bed and fiddled
   With a dreamland viol and bow,
And the tunes flew back to my fingers
   I had melodied years ago.
5  It was two or three in the morning
   When I fancy-fiddled so
Long reels and country-dances,
   And hornpipes swift and slow.

And soon anon came crossing
10   The chamber in the gray
Figures of jigging fieldfolk—
   Saviours of corn and hay—

To the air of "Haste to the Wedding,"
　　As after a wedding-day;
15　Yea, up and down the middle
　　In windless whirls went they!

There danced the bride and bridegroom,
　　And couples in a train,
Gay partners time and travail
20　　Had longwhiles stilled amain! . . .
It seemed a thing for weeping
　　To find, at slumber's wane
And morning's sly increeping,
　　That Now, not Then, held reign.


## The Dream Is—Which?

I am laughing by the brook with her,
　　Splashed in its tumbling stir;
And then it is a blankness looms
　　As if I walked not there,
5　Nor she, but found me in haggard rooms,
　　And treading a lonely stair.

With radiant cheeks and rapid eyes
　　We sit where none espies;
Till a harsh change comes edging in
10　　As no such scene were there,
But winter, and I were bent and thin,
　　And cinder-gray my hair.

We dance in heys around the hall,
　　Weightless as thistleball;
15　And then a curtain drops between,
　　As if I danced not there,
But wandered through a mounded green
　　To find her, I knew where.

## LONELY DAYS

Lonely her fate was,
Environed from sight
In the house where the gate was
Past finding at night.
5  None there to share it,
No one to tell:
Long she'd to bear it,
And bore it well.


Elsewhere just so she
10  Spent many a day;
Wishing to go she
Continued to stay.
And people without
Basked warm in the air,
15  But none sought her out,
Or knew she was there.
Even birthdays were passed so,
Sunny and shady:
Years did it last so
20  For this sad lady.
Never declaring it,
No one to tell,
Still she kept bearing it—
Bore it well.


25  The days grew chillier,
And then she went
To a city, familiar
In years forespent,
When she walked gaily

30    Far to and fro,
     But now, moving frailly,
     Could nowhere go.
     The cheerful colour
     Of houses she'd known
35    Had died to a duller
     And dingier tone.
     Streets were now noisy
     Where once had rolled
     A few quiet coaches,
40    Or citizens strolled.
     Through the party-wall
     Of the memoried spot
     They danced at a ball
     Who recalled her not.
45    Tramlines lay crossing
     Once gravelled slopes,
     Metal rods clanked,
     And electric ropes.
     So she endured it all,
50    Thin, thinner wrought,
     Until time cured it all,
     And she knew nought.

## THE MARBLE TABLET

There it stands, though alas, what a little of her
    Shows in its cold white look!
Not her glance, glide, or smile; not a tittle of her
    Voice like the purl of a brook;
5       Not her thoughts, that you read like a book.

It may stand for her once in November
    When first she breathed, witless of all;
Or in heavy years she would remember
    When circumstance held her in thrall;
10    Or at last, when she answered her call!

Nothing more. The still marble, date-graven,
    Gives all that it can, tersely lined;
That one has at length found the haven
    Which every one other will find;
15    With silence on what shone behind.

*St. Juliot: 8 September 1916*

## THE MASTER AND THE LEAVES

### I

We are budding, Master, budding,
    We of your favourite tree;
March drought and April flooding
    Arouse us merrily,
5  Our stemlets newly studding;
    And yet you do not see!

### II

We are fully woven for summer
    In stuff of limpest green,
The twitterer and the hummer
10    Here rest of nights, unseen,
While like a long-roll drummer
    The nightjar thrills the treen.

## III

We are turning yellow, Master,
 And next we are turning red,
15 And faster then and faster
 Shall seek our rooty bed,
All wasted in disaster!
 But you lift not your head.


## IV

—"I mark your early going,
20  And that you'll soon be clay,
I have seen your summer showing
 As in my youthful day;
But why I seem unknowing
 Is too sunk in to say!"


## LAST WORDS TO A DUMB FRIEND

Pet was never mourned as you,
Purrer of the spotless hue,
Plumy tail, and wistful gaze
While you humoured our queer ways,
5 Or outshrilled your morning call
Up the stairs and through the hall—
Foot suspended in its fall—
While, expectant, you would stand
Arched, to meet the stroking hand;
10 Till your way you chose to wend
Yonder, to your tragic end.

Never another pet for me!
Let your place all vacant be;
Better blankness day by day
Than companion torn away.
Better bid his memory fade,
Better blot each mark he made,
Selfishly escape distress
By contrived forgetfulness,
Than preserve his prints to make
Every morn and eve an ache.

From the chair whereon he sat
Sweep his fur, nor wince thereat;
Rake his little pathways out
Mid the bushes roundabout;
Smooth away his talons' mark
From the claw-worn pine-tree bark,
Where he climbed as dusk embrowned,
Waiting us who loitered round.

Strange it is this speechless thing,
Subject to our mastering,
Subject for his life and food
To our gift, and time, and mood;
Timid pensioner of us Powers,
His existence ruled by ours,
Should—by crossing at a breath
Into safe and shielded death,
By the merely taking hence
Of his insignificance—
Loom as largened to the sense,
Shape as part, above man's will,
Of the Imperturbable.

As a prisoner, flight debarred,
Exercising in a yard,
45  Still retain I, troubled, shaken,
Mean estate, by him forsaken;
And this home, which scarcely took
Impress from his little look,
By his faring to the Dim
50  Grows all eloquent of him.

Housemate, I can think you still
Bounding to the window-sill,
Over which I vaguely see
Your small mound beneath the tree,
55  Showing in the autumn shade
That you moulder where you played.


AN ANCIENT TO ANCIENTS

Where once we danced, where once we sang,
        Gentlemen,
The floors are sunken, cobwebs hang,
And cracks creep; worms have fed upon
5   The doors. Yea, sprightlier times were then
Than now, with harps and tabrets gone,
        Gentlemen!

Where once we rowed, where once we sailed,
        Gentlemen,
10  And damsels took the tiller, veiled
Against too strong a stare (God wot
Their fancy, then or anywhen!)
Upon that shore we are clean forgot,
        Gentlemen!

We have lost somewhat, afar and near,
        Gentlemen,
The thinning of our ranks each year
Affords a hint we are nigh undone,
That we shall not be ever again
The marked of many, loved of one,
        Gentlemen.

In dance the polka hit our wish,
        Gentlemen,
The paced quadrille, the spry schottische,
"Sir Roger."—And in opera spheres
The "Girl" (the famed "Bohemian"),
And "Trovatore," held the ears,
        Gentlemen.

This season's paintings do not please,
        Gentlemen,
Like Etty, Mulready, Maclise;
Throbbing romance has waned and wanned;
No wizard wields the witching pen
Of Bulwer, Scott, Dumas, and Sand,
        Gentlemen.

The bower we shrined to Tennyson,
        Gentlemen,
Is roof-wrecked; damps there drip upon
Sagged seats, the creeper-nails are rust,
The spider is sole denizen;
Even she who voiced those rhymes is dust,
        Gentlemen!

We who met sunrise sanguine-souled,
        Gentlemen,
Are wearing weary. We are old;

These younger press; we feel our rout
Is imminent to Aïdes' den,—
That evening shades are stretching out,
     Gentlemen!

50 And yet, though ours be failing frames,
     Gentlemen,
So were some others' history names,
Who trode their track light-limbed and fast
As these youth, and not alien
55 From enterprise, to their long last,
     Gentlemen.

Sophocles, Plato, Socrates,
     Gentlemen,
Pythagoras, Thucydides,
60 Herodotus, and Homer,—yea,
Clement, Augustin, Origen,
Burnt brightlier towards their setting-day,
     Gentlemen.

And ye, red-lipped and smooth-browed; list,
65      Gentlemen;
Much is there waits you we have missed;
Much lore we leave you worth the knowing,
Much, much has lain outside our ken:
Nay, rush not: time serves: we are going,
70      Gentlemen.

From
HUMAN SHOWS,
FAR PHANTASIES,
SONGS AND TRIFLES

## Waiting Both

A star looks down at me,
And says: "Here I and you
Stand, each in his degree:
What do you mean to do,—
        Mean to do?"

I say: "For all I know,
Wait, and let Time go by,
Till my change come."—"Just so,"
The star says: "So mean I:—
        So mean I."


## A Bird-Scene at a Rural Dwelling

When the inmate stirs, the birds retire discreetly
From the window-ledge, whereon they whistled sweetly
        And on the step of the door,
        In the misty morning hoar;
    But now the dweller is up they flee
        To the crooked neighbouring codlin-tree;
And when he comes fully forth they seek the garden,
And call from the lofty costard, as pleading pardon
        For shouting so near before
        In their joy at being alive:—
Meanwhile the hammering clock within goes five.

I know a domicile of brown and green,
Where for a hundred summers there have been
Just such enactments, just such daybreaks seen.

# Coming Up Oxford Street: Evening

The sun from the west glares back,
And the sun from the watered track,
And the sun from the sheets of glass,
And the sun from each window-brass;
5      Sun-mirrorings, too, brighten
From show-cases beneath
The laughing eyes and teeth
Of ladies who rouge and whiten.
And the same warm god explores
10      Panels and chinks of doors;
Problems with chymists' bottles
Profound as Aristotle's
He solves, and with good cause,
Having been ere man was.


15  Also he dazzles the pupils of one who walks west,
A city-clerk, with eyesight not of the best,
Who sees no escape to the very verge of his days
From the rut of Oxford Street into open ways;
And he goes along with head and eyes flagging forlorn,
20  Empty of interest in things, and wondering why he was born.


# When Dead

It will be much better when
    I am under the bough;
I shall be more myself, Dear, then,
    Than I am now.

No sign of querulousness
    To wear you out
Shall I show there: strivings and stress
    Be quite without.

This fleeting life-brief blight
    Will have gone past
When I resume my old and right
    Place in the Vast.

And when you come to me
    To show you true,
Doubt not I shall infallibly
    Be waiting you.


## TEN YEARS SINCE

    'Tis ten years since
  I saw her on the stairs,
  Heard her in house-affairs,
  And listened to her cares;
And the trees are ten feet taller,
And the sunny spaces smaller
Whose bloomage would enthrall her;
And the piano wires are rustier,
The smell of bindings mustier,
And lofts and lumber dustier
    Than when, with casual look
    And ear, light note I took
    Of what shut like a book
      Those ten years since!

*November 1922*

# LIFE AND DEATH AT SUNRISE

The hills uncap their tops
Of woodland, pasture, copse,
And look on the layers of mist
At their foot that still persist:
5 They are like awakened sleepers on one elbow lifted,
Who gaze around to learn if things during night have shifted.

A waggon creaks up from the fog
With a laboured leisurely jog;
Then a horseman from off the hill-tip
10 Comes clapping down into the dip;
While woodlarks, finches, sparrows, try to entune at one
time,
And cocks and hens and cows and bulls take up the chime.

With a shouldered basket and flagon
A man meets the one with the waggon,
15 And both the men halt of long use.
"Well," the waggoner says, "what's the news?"
"—'Tis a boy this time. You've just met the doctor trotting
back.
She's doing very well. And we think we shall call him 'Jack.'

"And what have you got covered there?"
20 He nods to the waggon and mare.
"Oh, a coffin for old John Thinn:
We are just going to put him in."
"—So he's gone at last. He always had a good constitution."
"—He was ninety-odd. He could call up the French
Revolution."

# A Sheep Fair

The day arrives of the autumn fair,
    And torrents fall,
Though sheep in throngs are gathered there,
    Ten thousand all,
5  Sodden, with hurdles round them reared:
And, lot by lot, the pens are cleared,
And the auctioneer wrings out his beard,
And wipes his book, bedrenched and smeared,
And rakes the rain from his face with the edge of his hand,
10      As torrents fall.

The wool of the ewes is like a sponge
    With the daylong rain:
Jammed tight, to turn, or lie, or lunge,
    They strive in vain.
15  Their horns are soft as finger-nails,
Their shepherds reek against the rails,
The tied dogs soak with tucked-in tails,
The buyers' hat-brims fill like pails,
Which spill small cascades when they shift their stand
20      In the daylong rain.

*Postscript*
Time has trailed lengthily since met
    At Pummery Fair
Those panting thousands in their wet
    And woolly wear:
25  And every flock long since has bled,
And all the dripping buyers have sped,
And the hoarse auctioneer is dead,
Who "Going—going!" so often said,
As he consigned to doom each meek, mewed band
30      At Pummery Fair.

## THE CALF

You may have seen, in road or street
    At times, when passing by,
A creature with bewildered bleat
Behind a milcher's tail, whose feet
5     Went pit-pat. That was I.

Whether we are of Devon kind,
    Shorthorns, or Herefords,
We are in general of one mind
That in the human race we find
10    Our masters and our lords.

When grown up (if they let me live)
    And in a dairy-home,
I may less wonder and misgive
Than now, and get contemplative,
15    And never wish to roam.

And in some fair stream, taking sips,
    May stand through summer noons,
With water dribbling from my lips
And rising halfway to my hips,
20    And babbling pleasant tunes.

## SNOW IN THE SUBURBS

      Every branch big with it,
       Bent every twig with it;
    Every fork like a white web-foot;
    Every street and pavement mute:
Some flakes have lost their way, and grope back upward,
                         when
Meeting those meandering down they turn and descend
                         again.
  The palings are glued together like a wall,
  And there is no waft of wind with the fleecy fall.

      A sparrow enters the tree,
       Whereon immediately
    A snow-lump thrice his own slight size
    Descends on him and showers his head and eyes,
        And overturns him,
        And near inurns him,
        And lights on a nether twig, when its brush
Starts off a volley of other lodging lumps with a rush.

      The steps are a blanched slope,
      Up which, with feeble hope,
    A black cat comes, wide-eyed and thin;
      And we take him in.

## ICE ON THE HIGHWAY

Seven buxom women abreast, and arm in arm,
    Trudge down the hill, tip-toed,
      And breathing warm;
They must perforce trudge thus, to keep upright
5    On the glassy ice-bound road,
And they must get to market whether or no,
    Provisions running low
    With the nearing Saturday night,
While the lumbering van wherein they mostly ride
10    Can nowise go:
Yet loud their laughter as they stagger and slide!


## NO BUYERS
*A Street Scene*

A load of brushes and baskets and cradles and chairs
    Labours along the street in the rain:
With it a man, a woman, a pony with whiteybrown
          hairs.—
    The man foots in front of the horse with a shambling
          sway
5    At a slower tread than a funeral train,
    While to a dirge-like tune he chants his wares,
Swinging a Turk's-head brush (in a drum-major's way
    When the bandsmen march and play).

A yard from the back of the man is the whiteybrown pony's
                                                          nose:
10  He mirrors his master in every item of pace and pose:
            He stops when the man stops, without being told,
                And seems to be eased by a pause; too plainly he's old,
                    Indeed, not strength enough shows
                To steer the disjointed waggon straight,
15          Which wriggles left and right in a rambling line,
            Deflected thus by its own warp and weight,
            And pushing the pony with it in each incline.

                The woman walks on the pavement verge,
                    Parallel to the man:
20          She wears an apron white and wide in span,
        And carries a like Turk's-head, but more in nursing-wise:
                Now and then she joins in his dirge,
                But as if her thoughts were on distant things.
                The rain clams her apron till it clings.—
25          So, step by step, they move with their merchandize,
                And nobody buys.


ONE WHO MARRIED ABOVE HIM

        " 'Tis you, I think? Back from your week's work,
                                                    Steve?"

    "It is I. Back from work this Christmas Eve."

    "But you seem off again?—in this night-rime?"

    "I am off again, and thoroughly off this time."

5       "What does that mean?"

"More than may first be seen. . . .
　　Half an hour ago I footed homeward here,
　　No wife found I, nor child, nor maid, indoors or near.
　She has, as always, gone with them to her mother's at the
　　　　　　　　　　　　　　　farm,
Where they fare better far than here, and, maybe, meet less
　　　　　　　　　　　　　　　harm.
　　She's left no fire, no light, has cooked me nothing to eat,
　　Though she had fuel, and money to get some Christmas
　　　　　　　　　　　　　　　meat.
　　Christmas with them is grand, she knows, and brings good
　　　　　　　　　　　　　　　victual,
　　Other than how it is here, where it's but lean and little.
　　　　But though not much, and rough,
　　　　If managed neat there's enough.
　　She and hers are too highmade for me;
　　But she's whimmed her once too often, she'll see!
Farmer Bollen's daughter should never have married a man
　　　　　　　　　　　　　　　that's poor;
And I can stand it no longer; I'm leaving; you'll see me no
　　　　　　　　　　　　　　　more, be sure."


"But nonsense: you'll be back again ere bedtime, and
　　　　　　　　　　　　　　　lighting a fire,
And sizzling your supper, and vexing not that her views of
　　　　　　　　　　　　　　　supper are higher."
　　　　"Never for me."


　　　　"Well, we shall see."


The sceptical neighbour and Stephen then followed their
　　　　　　　　　　　　　　　foredesigned ways,
And their steps dimmed into white silence upon the slippery
　　　　　　　　　　　　　　　glaze;
And the trees went on with their spitting amid the icicled
　　　　　　　　　　　　　　　haze.

The evening whiled, and the wife with the babies came
                                    home,
But he was not there, nor all Christmas Day did he come.
Christmastide went, and likewise went the New Year,
    But no husband's footfall revived,
And month after month lapsed, graytime to green and to
                                    sere,
    And other new years arrived,
And the children grew up: one husbanded and one
                                    wived.—
        She wept and repented,
    But Stephen never relented.
And there stands the house, and the sycamore-tree and all,
With its roots forming steps for the passers who care to call,
    And there are the mullioned windows, and Ham-Hill
                                    door,
Through which Steve's wife was brought out, but which
                            Steve re-entered no more.


LAST LOVE-WORD

This is the last; the very, very last!
        Anon, and all is dead and dumb,
        Only a pale shroud over the past,
                That cannot be
        Of value small or vast,
                Love, then to me!

I can say no more: I have even said too much.
        I did not mean that this should come:
        I did not know 'twould swell to such—
                Nor, perhaps, you—
        When that first look and touch,
                Love, doomed us two!

## Nobody Comes

Tree-leaves labour up and down,
  And through them the fainting light
  Succumbs to the crawl of night.
Outside in the road the telegraph wire
   To the town from the darkening land
Intones to travellers like a spectral lyre
  Swept by a spectral hand.

A car comes up, with lamps full-glare,
  That flash upon a tree:
  It has nothing to do with me,
And whangs along in a world of its own,
  Leaving a blacker air;
And mute by the gate I stand again alone,
  And nobody pulls up there.

*October 9, 1924*


## When Oats Were Reaped

That day when oats were reaped, and wheat was ripe, and
       barley ripening,
  The road-dust hot, and the bleaching grasses dry,
   I walked along and said,
While looking just ahead to where some silent people lie:

"I wounded one who's there, and now know well I
       wounded her;
  But, ah, she does not know that she wounded me!"
   And not an air stirred,
Nor a bill of any bird; and no response accorded she.

*August 1913*

## THE HARBOUR BRIDGE

From here, the quay, one looks above to mark
The bridge across the harbour, hanging dark
Against the day's-end sky, fair-green in glow
Over and under the middle archway's bow:
5  It draws its skeleton where the sun has set,
Yea, clear from cutwater to parapet;
On which mild glow, too, lines of rope and spar
      Trace themselves black as char.

Down here in shade we hear the painters shift
10  Against the bollards with a drowsy lift,
As moved by the incoming stealthy tide.
High up across the bridge the burghers glide
As cut black-paper portraits hastening on
In conversation none knows what upon:
15  Their sharp-edged lips move quickly word by word
      To speech that is not heard.

There trails the dreamful girl, who leans and stops,
There presses the practical woman to the shops,
There is a sailor, meeting his wife with a start,
20  And we, drawn nearer, judge they are keeping apart.
Both pause. She says: "I've looked for you. I thought
We'd make it up." Then no words can be caught.
At last: "Won't you come home?" She moves still nigher:
     " 'Tis comfortable, with a fire."

25  "No," he says gloomily. "And, anyhow,
I can't give up the other woman now:
You should have talked like that in former days,
When I was last home." They go different ways.

And the west dims, and yellow lamplights shine:
30    And soon above, like lamps more opaline,
White stars ghost forth, that care not for men's wives,
        Or any other lives.

                                                        *Weymouth*


## THE MISSED TRAIN

            How I was caught
Hieing home, after days of allure,
And forced to an inn—small, obscure—
        At the junction, gloom-fraught.

5           How civil my face
To get them to chamber me there—
A roof I had scorned, scarce aware
        That it stood at the place.

        And how all the night
10   I had dreams of the unwitting cause
Of my lodgment. How lonely I was;
        How consoled by her sprite!

        Thus onetime to me . . .
Dim wastes of dead years bar away
15   Then from now. But such happenings to-day
        Fall to lovers, may be!

        Years, years as shoaled seas,
Truly, stretch now between! Less and less
Shrink the visions then vast in me.—Yes,
20       Then in me: Now in these.

## RETTY'S PHASES

### I

Retty used to shake her head,
    Look with wicked eye;
Say, "I'd tease you, simple Ned,
    If I cared to try!"
Then she'd hot-up scarlet red,
    Stilly step away,
Much afraid that what she'd said
    Sounded bold to say.

### II

Retty used to think she loved
    (Just a little) me.
Not untruly, as it proved
    Afterwards to be.
For, when weakness forced her rest
    If we walked a mile,
She would whisper she was blest
    By my clasp awhile.

### III

Retty used at last to say
    When she neared the Vale,
"Mind that you, Dear, on that day
    Ring my wedding peal!"
And we all, with pulsing pride,
    Vigorous sounding gave
Those six bells, the while outside
    John filled in her grave.

25 Retty used to draw me down
    To the turfy heaps,
Where, with yeoman, squire, and clown
    Noticeless she sleeps.
Now her silent slumber-place
30     Seldom do I know,
For when last I saw her face
    Was so long ago!


## THE SUNDIAL ON A WET DAY

I drip, drip here
In Atlantic rain,
Falling like handfuls
Of winnowed grain,
5 Which, tear-like, down
My gnomon drain,
And dim my numerals
With their stain,—
Till I feel useless,
10 And wrought in vain!

And then I think
In my despair
That, though unseen,
*He* is still up there,
15 And may gaze out
Anywhen, anywhere;
Not to help clockmen
Quiz and compare,
But in kindness to let me
20 My trade declare.

## SHORTENING DAYS AT THE HOMESTEAD

The first fire since the summer is lit, and is smoking into the
                                                    room:
   The sun-rays thread it through, like woof-lines in a loom.
   Sparrows spurt from the hedge, whom misgivings appal
That winter did not leave last year for ever, after all.
   Like shock-headed urchins, spiny-haired,
   Stand pollard willows, their twigs just bared.

   Who is this coming with pondering pace,
   Black and ruddy, with white embossed,
   His eyes being black, and ruddy his face,
   And the marge of his hair like morning frost?
         It's the cider-maker,
         And appletree-shaker,
And behind him on wheels, in readiness,
His mill, and tubs, and vat, and press.

## A Hurried Meeting

It is August moonlight in the tall plantation,
Whose elms, by aged squirrels' footsteps worn,
   Outscreen the noon, and eve, and morn.
On the facing slope a faint irradiation
5    From a mansion's marble front is borne,
     Mute in its woodland wreathing.
    Up here the night-jar whirrs forlorn,
And the trees seem to withhold their softest breathing.

To the moonshade slips a woman in muslin vesture:
10 Her naked neck the gossamer-web besmears,
    And she sweeps it away with a hasty gesture.
Again it touches her forehead, her neck, her ears,
     Her fingers, the backs of her hands.
     She sweeps it away again
15    Impatiently, and then
She takes no notice; and listens, and sighs, and stands.

The night-hawk stops. A man shows in the obscure:
     They meet, and passively kiss,
And he says: "Well, I've come quickly. About this—
20    Is it really so? You are sure?"
   "I am sure. In February it will be.
   That such a thing should come to me!
We should have known. We should have left off meeting.
Love is a terrible thing: a sweet allure
25    That ends in heart-outeating!"

"But what shall we do, my Love, and how?"
"You need not call me by that name now."
Then he more coldly: "What is your suggestion?"
"I've told my mother, and she sees a way,
Since of our marriage there can be no question.
We are crossing South—near about New Year's Day
    The event will happen there.
It is the only thing that we can dare
    To keep them unaware!"
    "Well, you can marry me."
She shook her head. "No: that can never be.

" 'Twill be brought home as hers. She's forty-one,
When many a woman's bearing is not done,
    And well might have a son.—
We should have left off specious self-deceiving:
    I feared that such might come,
    And knowledge struck me numb.
Love is a terrible thing: witching when first begun,
    To end in grieving, grieving!"

And with one kiss again the couple parted:
Inferior clearly he; she haughty-hearted.
He watched her down the slope to return to her place,
The marble mansion of her ancient race,
And saw her brush the gossamers from her face
As she emerged from shade to the moonlight ray.
    And when she had gone away
  The night-jar seemed to imp, and say,
    "You should have taken warning:
Love is a terrible thing: sweet for a space,
    And then all mourning, mourning!"

## A Leaving

Knowing what it bore
I watched the rain-smitten back of the car—
(Brown-curtained, such as the old ones were)—
When it started forth for a journey afar
5      Into the sullen November air,
And passed the glistening laurels and round the bend.

I have seen many gayer vehicles turn that bend
In autumn, winter, and summer air,
Bearing for journeys near or afar
10      Many who now are not, but were,
But I don't forget that rain-smitten car,
Knowing what it bore!

From
WINTER WORDS
IN VARIOUS MOODS
AND METRES

## Proud Songsters

The thrushes sing as the sun is going,
And the finches whistle in ones and pairs,
And as it gets dark loud nightingales
      In bushes
5  Pipe, as they can when April wears,
      As if all Time were theirs.

These are brand new birds of twelvemonths' growing,
Which a year ago, or less than twain,
No finches were, nor nightingales,
10        Nor thrushes,
But only particles of grain,
      And earth, and air, and rain.


## "I Am the One"

I am the one whom ringdoves see
      Through chinks in boughs
5        When they do not rouse
      In sudden dread,
But stay on cooing, as if they said:
      "Oh; it's only he."

I am the passer when up-eared hares,
10        Stirred as they eat
      The new-sprung wheat,
      Their munch resume
As if they thought: "He is one for whom
      Nobody cares."

15  Wet-eyed mourners glance at me
          As in train they pass
          Along the grass
          To a hollowed spot,
    And think: "No matter; he quizzes not
20        Our misery."

    I hear above: "We stars must lend
          No fierce regard
          To his gaze, so hard
          Bent on us thus,—
25  Must scathe him not. He is one with us
          Beginning and end."


## EXPECTATION AND EXPERIENCE

    "I had a holiday once," said the woman—
        Her name I did not know—
    "And I thought that where I'd like to go,
    Of all the places for being jolly,
5   And getting rid of melancholy,
        Would be to a good big fair:
    And I went. And it rained in torrents, drenching
    Every horse, and sheep, and yeoman,
        And my shoulders, face, and hair;
10  And I found that I was the single woman
        In the field—and looked quite odd there!
    Everything was spirit-quenching:
    I crept and stood in the lew of a wall
    To think, and could not tell at all
15      What on earth made me plod there!"

## THROWING A TREE

The two executioners stalk along over the knolls,
Bearing two axes with heavy heads shining and wide,
And a long limp two-handled saw toothed for cutting
                    great boles,
And so they approach the proud tree that bears the death-
                    mark on its side.

Jackets doffed they swing axes and chop away just above
                    ground,
And the chips fly about and lie white on the moss and
                    fallen leaves;
Till a broad deep gash in the bark is hewn all the way
                    round,
And one of them tries to hook upward a rope, which at last
                    he achieves.

The saw then begins, till the top of the tall giant shivers:
The shivers are seen to grow greater each cut than
                    before:
They edge out the saw, tug the rope; but the tree only
                    quivers,
And kneeling and sawing again, they step back to try pulling
                    once more.

Then, lastly, the living mast sways, further sways: with
                    a shout
Job and Ike rush aside. Reached the end of its long
                    staying powers
The tree crashes downward: it shakes all its neighbours
                    throughout,
And two hundred years steady growth has been ended in less
                    than two hours.

## Lying Awake

You, Morningtide Star, now are steady-eyed, over the east,
    I know it as if I saw you;
You, Beeches, engrave on the sky your thin twigs, even the
                         least;
    Had I paper and pencil I'd draw you.

5  You, Meadow, are white with your counterpane cover of
                         dew,
    I see it as if I were there;
You, Churchyard, are lightening faint from the shade of the
                         yew,
    The names creeping out everywhere.


## Henley Regatta

She looks from the window: still it pours down direly,
And the avenue drips. She cannot go, she fears;
And the Regatta will be spoilt entirely;
    And she sheds half-crazed tears.

5  Regatta Day and rain come on together
Again, years after. Gutters trickle loud;
But Nancy cares not. She knows nought of weather,
    Or of the Henley crowd:

She's a Regatta quite her own. Inanely
10  She laughs in the asylum as she floats
Within a water-tub, which she calls "Henley,"
    Her little paper boats.

## "A Gentleman's Second-Hand Suit"

Here it is hanging in the sun
    By the pawn-shop door,
A dress-suit—all its revels done
    Of heretofore.
Long drilled to the waltzers' swing and sway,
    As its tokens show:
What it has seen, what it could say
    If it did but know!

The sleeve bears still a print of powder
    Rubbed from her arms
When she warmed up as the notes swelled louder
    And livened her charms—
Or rather theirs, for beauties many
    Leant there, no doubt,
Leaving these tell-tale traces when he
    Spun them about.

Its cut seems rather in bygone style
    On looking close,
So it mayn't have bent it for some while
    To the dancing pose:
Anyhow, often within its clasp
    Fair partners hung,
Assenting to the wearer's grasp
    With soft sweet tongue.

Where is, alas, the gentleman
    Who wore this suit?
And where are his ladies? Tell none can:
    Gossip is mute.
Some of them may forget him quite
    Who smudged his sleeve,
Some think of a wild and whirling night
    With him, and grieve.

# A Forgotten Miniature

There you are in the dark,
    Deep in a box
Nobody ever unlocks,
Or even turns to mark;
5      —Out of mind stark.

Yet there you have not been worsed
    Like your sitter
By Time, the Fair's hard-hitter;
Your beauties, undispersed,
10    Glow as at first.

Shut in your case for years,
    Never an eye
Of the many passing nigh,
Fixed on their own affairs,
15    Thinks what it nears!

—While you have lain in gloom,
    A form forgot,
Your reign remembered not,
Much life has come to bloom
20    Within this room.

Yea, in Time's cyclic sweep
    Unrest has ranged:
Women and men have changed:
Some you knew slumber deep;
25    Some wait for sleep.

# APPENDIX: HARDY'S NOTES AND REMARKS

Discursive prose was not Hardy's natural medium, but he had cogent, interesting, and penetrating things to say, on the art of poetry as well as on other matters. What follows are various comments and jottings from notebooks, letters, conversations, and, in one case, from a novel. When he speaks of himself in the third person, the quotation comes from his autobiography (which was published under the name of his second wife and intended to be taken as a biography). I give dates only when they seem important; my own occasional comments are in bracketed italics.

The jewelled line is effeminate.

The business of the poet and novelist is to show the sorriness underlying the grandest things, and the grandeur underlying the sorriest things.

The whole secret of a living style and the difference between it and a dead style, lies in not having too much style—being, in fact, a little careless, or rather seeming to be, here and there. It brings wonderful life into the writing. . . .

   *[and is very annoying to readers like T. S. Eliot]*

Arnold *[Matthew Arnold],* according to Hardy's account of their meeting much later, "had a manner of having made up his mind upon everything years ago, so that it was a pleasing futility for his interlocutor to begin thinking new ideas, different from his own, at that time of day." Yet he was frank and modest enough to assure Hardy deprecatingly that he was only a hard-worked school-inspector.

Arnold is wrong about provincialism, if he means anything
more than a provincialism of style and manner in exposi-
tion. A certain provincialism of feeling is invaluable. It is
of the essence of individuality.

Poetry is emotion put into measure. The emotion must
come by nature, but the measure can be acquired by art.
. . . That the author loved the art of concealing art was
undiscerned. For instance, as to rhythm. Years earlier he
had decided that too regular a beat was bad art. . . . He
knew that in architecture cunning irregularity is of enor-
mous worth, and it is obvious that he carried on into
his verse, perhaps in part unconsciously, the Gothic art-
principle in which he had been trained—the principle of
spontaneity found in mouldings, tracery, and such like—
resulting in the "unforeseen" (as it has been called) char-
acter of his metres and stanzas, that of stress rather than of
syllable, poetic texture rather than poetic veneer. . . .

The artistic spirit is at bottom a spirit of caprice, and in
some of its finest productions in the past it could have
given no clear reason why they were run in this or that
particular mould, and not in some more obvious one.

I hold that the mission of poetry is to record impressions,
not convictions. Wordsworth in his later writings fell into
the error of recording the latter. So also did Tennyson, and
so do many poets when they grow old. *Absit omen!*
    [*"Absit omen" means "Let it not be an omen," or as we
might say, "Knock on wood."*]

Unadjusted impressions have their value, and the road to
a true philosophy of life seems to lie in humbly recording
diverse readings of its phenomena as they are forced upon
us by chance and change.

The following note on London at dawn occurs on
May 19 *[1880]*, a night on which he could not sleep, partly
on account of an eerie feeling which sometimes haunted

him, a horror at lying down in close proximity to "a monster whose body had four million heads and eight million eyes."

". . . This hum of the wheel—the roar of London! What is it composed of? Hurry, speech, laughters, moans, cries of little children. The people in this tragedy laugh, sing, smoke, toss off wines, etc., make love to girls in drawing-rooms and areas; and yet are playing their part in the tragedy just the same. Some wear jewels and feathers, some wear rags. All are caged birds; the only difference lies in the size of the cage. This too is part of the tragedy."

June 2 *[1887].* The forty-seventh birthday of Thomas the Unworthy.

That girl in the omnibus had one of those faces of marvelous beauty which are seen casually in the streets but never among one's friends. . . . Where do these women come from? Who marries them? Who knows them?

Christmas Day *[1890].* While thinking of resuming "the viewless wings of poesy" before dawn this morning, new horizons seemed to open and worrying pettinesses to disappear.

In the early weeks of this year *[1900]* the poems were reviewed in the customary periodicals—mostly in a friendly tone, even in a tone of respect, and with some praise for many pieces in the volume; though by some critics not without umbrage at Hardy's having taken the liberty to adopt another vehicle of expression than prose-fiction without consulting them.

The "simply natural" is interesting no longer. The much decried, mad, late-Turner rendering is now necessary to create my interest.

For my part, if there is any way of getting a melancholy satisfaction out of life, it lies in dying, so to speak, before one is out of the flesh; by which I mean putting on the manners of ghosts, wandering in their haunts, and taking their views of surrounding things. To think of life as passing away is a sadness; to think of it as past is at least tolerable. Hence even when I enter into a room to pay a simple morning call I have unconsciously the habit of regarding the scene as if I were a spectre not solid enough to influence my environment; only fit to behold and say, as another spectre said: "Peace be unto you!"

The poet is like one who enters and mounts a platform to give an address as announced. He opens his page, looks around, and finds the hall—*empty*.

To find beauty in ugliness is the province of the poet.

POETRY. Perhaps I can express more fully in verse ideas and emotions which run counter to the inert crystalized opinion—hard as a rock—which the vast body of men have vested interests in supporting. . . . If Galileo had said in verse that the world moved, the Inquisition might have let him alone.

The besetting sin of modern literature is its insincerity.

The thoughts of any man of letters concerned to keep poetry alive cannot but run uncomfortably on the precarious prospects of English verse at the present day. . . . Whether owing to the barbarizing of taste in the younger minds by the dark madness of the late war, the unabashed cultivation of selfishness in all classes, the plethoric growth of knowledge simultaneously with the stunting of wisdom, "a degrading thirst after outrageous stimulation" (to quote Wordsworth), or from any other cause, we seem threatened with a new Dark Age.

I am most anxious to believe in what, roughly speaking, we may call the supernatural—but I find no evidence for it. People accuse me of scepticism, materialism, and so forth; but, if the accusation is just at all, it is quite against my will. . . . I would give ten years of my life—well, perhaps that offer is rather beyond my means—but when I was a younger man, I would cheerfully have given ten years of my life to see a ghost—an authentic, indubitable spectre. . . . Never the ghost of a ghost. Yet I should think I am cut out by nature for a ghost-seer. My nerves vibrate very readily; people say I am almost morbidly imaginative; my will to believe is perfect. If ever ghost wanted to manifest himself, I am the very man he should apply to. But no—the spirits don't seem to see it!

Have you ever noticed the different relation to nature of the town child and the country child? The town-bred boy will often appreciate nature more than the country boy, but he does not know it in the same sense. He will rush to pick a flower which the country boy does not seem to notice. But it is part of the country boy's life. It grows in his soul—he does not want it in his buttonhole.

Misapprehension. The shrinking soul thinks its weak place is going to be laid bare, and shows its thought by a suddenly clipped manner. The other shrinking soul thinks the clipped manner of the first to be the result of its own weakness in some way, not of its strength, and shows its fear also by its constrained air! So they withdraw from each other and misunderstand.

It would be an amusing fact, if it were not one that leads to such bitter strife, that the conception of a First Cause which the theist calls "God," and the conception of the same that the so-styled atheist calls "no-God," are nowadays almost exactly identical. So that only a minor literary question of terminology prevents their shaking hands in agreement, and dwelling together in unity ever after.

Much confusion has arisen and much nonsense has been talked latterly in connection with the word "atheist." I have never understood how anybody can be one except in the sense of disbelieving in a tribal god, man-shaped, fiery-faced and tyrannous, who flies into a rage on the slightest provocation.

You must not think me a hard-headed rationalist for all this. Half my time—particularly when writing verse—I "believe" (in the modern sense of the word) not only in the things Bergson believes in, but in spectres, mysterious voices, intuitions, omens, dreams, haunted places, etc., etc. But I do not believe in them in the old sense of the word. . . .

Swinburne told me that he read in some paper, "Swinburne planteth, Hardy watereth, and Satan giveth the increase."

"NO man is master of his soul; the flesh is the master of it!"
   *[He is speaking of W. E. Henley's "Invictus"]*

Some people would like to know whence the poet whose philosophy is in these days deemed as profound and trustworthy as his song is breezy and pure, gets his authority for speaking of Nature's 'holy plan.'
   *[He means Wordsworth.]*

A Pessimist's apology. Pessimism (or rather what is called such) is, in brief, playing the sure game. You cannot lose at it; you may gain. It is the only view of life in which you can never be disappointed. Having reckoned what to do in the worst possible circumstances, when better arise, as they may, life becomes child's play.

An author cannot always tell what people will like most. Posterity alone can decide. So I generally publish everything. When I have been in doubt (as I was, for example, with my last volume) about two or three poems, I afterward found that those were often what some people liked best; and poems I have been on the point of discarding have sometimes been used in anthologies. . . . What a number of anthologies there are now!

What made poetry 2000 years ago makes poetry now.

September 15 *[1914]*. Thoughts on the recent school of novel-writers. They forget in their insistence on life, and nothing but life, in a plain slice, that a story *must be worth the telling,* that a good deal of life is not worth any such thing, and that they must not occupy a reader's time with what he can get at first hand anywhere around him.

June 10 *[1923]*. Relativity. That things and events always were, are, and will be (*e.g.,* Emma, Mother and Father are living still in the past).

During this month, November *[1926]*, his friend, Colonel T. E. Lawrence, called to say good-bye, before starting for India. Hardy was much affected by this parting, as T. E. Lawrence was one of his most valued friends. He went into the little porch and stood at the front door to see the departure of Lawrence on his motor-bicycle. This machine was difficult to start, and, thinking he might have to wait some time Hardy turned into the house to fetch a shawl to wrap round him. In the meantime, fearing that Hardy might take a chill, Lawrence started the motor-bicycle and hurried away. Returning a few moments later, Hardy was grieved that he had not seen the actual departure. . . .

The value of old age depends upon the person who reaches it. To some men of early performance it is useless. To others, who are late to develop, it just enables them to complete their job.

I have . . . of late years lapsed so deeply into my early weakness for verse, and have found the condensed expression that it affords so much more consonant to my natural way of thinking and feeling—that I have almost forgotten the prose effusions for the time.

# NOTES

I have for the most part refrained from interpretation and from definitions that any good dictionary can supply. These notes are largely concerned with defining the rare, archaic, or dialect words that Hardy sometimes uses, untying the occasional knot of syntax, elucidating the less familiar allusions, and giving whatever background—biographical, historical, folkloric, technical, etc.— seems pertinent, useful, or interesting. When I could not help myself, I have commented on the beauties of this or that poem. Hardy's poetry is in general very accessible, and nearly half the poems in this selection do not, I think, require any annotation at all.

### Domicilium

1 It is not possible to date this poem exactly, but Hardy would have been little older than seventeen or eighteen when he wrote it. The blank verse, though obviously derivative of Wordsworth, is as good as any he ever did; in any case, it is remarkable work for a boy.

1.10 *esculent:* edible

2.34 *Heathcroppers:* ponies that graze on open downs

### WESSEX POEMS:

5–11 Hardy's Wessex is an imaginary region, rather like Faulkner's Yoknapatawpha County, that corresponds, roughly, to the land in which he was born and lived most of his life. He derived the name from the kingdom of the West Saxons, first using it in *Far from the Madding Crowd.* Years later he wrote the following description of this fictional landscape: ". . . the people in most of the novels (and in much of the shorter verse) are dwellers in a province bounded on the north by the Thames, on the south by the English Channel, on the east by a line running from Hayling Island to Windsor Forest, and on the west by the Cornish coast." The territory he defined so precisely embraces some sections of Wiltshire, Hampshire, Berkshire, Devon, Somerset, and Cornwall, but it is essentially Dorset. I shall identify here the names of the principal towns, parishes, and landmarks in the order that they appear in the selected poems, the fictional name followed by the real name (omitting minor or unimportant ones, or those whose names are too similar to mistake, such as the Frome River and the *Froom*).

*Mellstock:* Stinsford Parish (St. Michael's Church)
*Weatherbury:* Puddletown
*Durnover:* Fordington (*Durnovaria* was the old Roman name for Dorchester)
*Ivel:* Yeovil
*Casterbridge:* Dorchester
*Budmouth:* Weymouth
*Boterel:* Boscastle
*Pummery:* Poundbury Camp
(Stinsford, Puddletown, Fordington, and Poundbury Camp are all within a few miles of Dorchester. Poundbury Camp is an ancient hill-fort on a hill just outside of town. Yeovil is a little village in Blackmoor Vale, about ten miles north. Weymouth is on the coast, seven miles south.)

### Hap

5 That is, Chance (which was the original title). The sonnet is itself a definition of the word.

5.11 *Crass Casualty:* Hap; contingency [archaism]. Hardy was not pleased when *Crass* was taken to mean stupid or malign, rather than merely insensible: the fates are blind and their sentences are entirely random.

5.13 *Doomsters:* judges; agents of our destinies

### Friends Beyond

7 As in many of the poems, the characters are based on actual people that Hardy knew, or knew of—you can

find the graves of Farmer Bedloe and Robert Reason in the churchyard at Stinsford. Some of these people also appear in the novels. The meter is trochaic octameter, as in Tennyson's "Locksley Hall" and Browning's "A Toccata of Galuppi's." As usual, Hardy has devised a variant: the middle line of each tercet is a tetrameter, and the rhyme scheme, surprisingly, is *terza rima*—as John Crowe Ransom notes, "Dante's terza rima, a form exalted among university poets. We have attended a startling marriage between high and low" (the low being the native meter and the homely village folk).

7.1  *Tranter:* carrier who moves people's goods by horse and wagon [dialect]

7.6  *leads:* coverings of roofs

7.7  *fellow-wight:* fellow-creature [arch.]

7.9  *stillicide:* the dripping of water [rare]

8.17  *hold the manse in fee:* possess the mansion as a rightful and heritable estate [arch.]

8.21  *Quiz:* pry into, perhaps ridicule

8.23  *grinterns:* granary bins [dial.]

8.24  *ho:* grieve [dial.]

8.30  *City stage:* the London stagecoach

8.32  *the Trine:* the Trinity

8.33  *none witteth:* no one knows [arch.]—that is to say, who knows why God permits living creatures to suffer so?

8.33  *haps:* happens (See "Hap." It is probable that the old form of the verb retains more strongly the sense of chance and contingency.)

### Nature's Questioning

9  Always careful not to be held to ideas that are nothing more than speculations, Hardy wrote that the poem's notions of the godhead—the Automaton, the Vast Imbecility, the Plan—"are merely enumerated . . . as fanciful alternatives to several others, and have nothing to do with my own opinion."

*In a Eweleaze at Weatherbury*

10 *Eweleaze:* field in which sheep are pastured [dial.]

10.5–8 The last few lines of the first stanza suggest that the speaker might be a woman—possibly Hardy's cousin, Tryphena Sparks, who was trained as a teacher and later became headmistress of a school, and with whom Hardy is supposed to have been in love in their youth; she died in 1890, the date appended to the poem. But of course the poem could be read differently. (In many of Hardy's love poems—"Neutral Tones," for instance—we assume the speaker to be a man, a surrogate for the poet; a fair number—"Neutral Tones," for instance—could as easily be spoken by a woman.)

10.11 *Defacing wan and grizzel / The blazon of my prime:* damaging, by making lusterless and grey, the heraldic shield, and the vaunting, of my youth (and possibly its blazing out, by likeness of sound)

*Embarcation*

15 The Boer War began in October 1899; by the end of November, nearly 60,000 troops had sailed out of Southampton, bound for South Africa. (A waving hand is one of Hardy's characteristic images and is to be found in a number of poems—see "The Rejected Member's Wife," "Logs on the Hearth," and "The Last Signal.")

*Drummer Hodge*

15 Hardy's note (first magazine publication): "One of the Drummers killed was a native of a village near Casterbridge."

15.1 *Hodge:* patronizing generic name for a rustic laborer. In *Tess of the D'Urbervilles*, we read, "The conventional farm-folk of his imagination—personified in the newspaper-press by the pitiable dummy known as Hodge—were obliterated after a few days' residence. At close quarters no Hodge was to be seen. . . . He had been disintegrated into a number of varied fellow-creatures—beings of many minds, beings infinite in difference;

some happy, many serene, a few depressed, one here and there bright even to genius, some stupid, others wanton, others austere; some mutely Miltonic, some potentially Cromwellian; into men who had private views of each other, as he had of his friends. . . ."

15.3 *kopje:* small hill

15.4 *veldt:* grassy plain, savanna

16.9 *Karoo:* high arid plateau in South Africa

### The Souls of the Slain

16 Hardy's note (first magazine publication): "The spot indicated . . . is the Bill of Portland, which stands, roughly, on a line drawn from South Africa to the middle of the United Kingdom. . . . The 'Race' is the turbulent sea-area off the Bill, where contrary tides meet."

17.15 *mighty-vanned:* with great wings [poetical]

17.27 *nether bord:* lower border, or southernly frontier; here, below the Tropic of Capricorn—South Africa, of course

20.93 *Pentecost Wind:* Pentecost is the day the disciples were filled with the Holy Ghost and began to speak in tongues. See Acts 2: "And suddenly there came a sound from heaven as of a rushing mighty wind. . . ."

### Rome: At the Pyramid of Cestius Near the Graves of Shelley and Keats

21.1 *Cestius:* an obscure Roman tribune who lived in the first century before Christ

21.14 *breathed out threatening:* Acts 9:1

### Zermatt: To the Matterhorn

22.4 *four lives paid:* The Matterhorn was first climbed in July of 1865 by a party led by the famed Alpinist, Edward Whymper, later a friend of Hardy's. As they were coming down, four of the men slipped and fell some 4,000 feet to their death; Whymper and two others survived because the rope linking them to the four men broke.

The Hardys visited Zermatt in 1897, a few years after
Whymper had told him the tragic story.

22.14  *When darkness filled the earth till the ninth hour:*
Mark 15:33

### To an Unborn Pauper Child

22  On the manuscript Hardy wrote, below the title,
" 'She must go to the Union-house to have her baby.'
*Petty Sessions.*" (The Union-house was a workhouse for
people living on public charity.)

22.5  *teens:* harm inflicted or suffered, misery, rage [dial.]

22.6  *Time-wraiths:* specters caught in our temporal realm—
perhaps meaning people as thin and unsubstantial as
ghosts

23.25  *Fain:* gladly [arch.]

23.26  *wold:* wooded upland; tract of hilly uncultivated coun-
try [dial.]
There are many fine strokes in this poem—the first
line, for one, an iambic tetrameter in which six or
seven syllables, instead of the usual four, can be stressed;
*Must come and bide,* a powerful sentence—just the com-
pound verb, its subject unnamed; and Hardy's com-
passionate tenderness toward the imagined fetus, most
moving when he addresses it as "Dear."

### To Lizbie Browne

24  Lizbie Browne's real name was Elizabeth Bishop. She
was the daughter of a local gamekeeper.

26.52  *As not:* as no longer living; it may also suggest *like
as not.*

### At a Hasty Wedding

28  Many rural weddings took place when the bride was
well along in pregnancy. The title is perhaps privately
ironic: one of the joyous songs that Hardy and his fa-
ther played at such festivities was "Haste to the Wed-
ding." Hardy identified this poem as a triolet—the best
in English, in my opinion. He uses the brevity and
swiftness of the form and its inexorable repetitions to

express with great power both the urgency of desire and the certainty of change and loss. ("Winter in Durn-over Field" is written in the same difficult form.)

*An August Midnight*

30.4 *dumbledore:* some editors have identified this as the cockchafer beetle; the O.E.D. gives bumble-bee; in any case, a buzzing insect of some size.

*The Darkling Thrush*

33 Several scholars cite a passage from W. H. Hudson's *Nature in Downland* as one of the sources of this poem:

> Mid-winter is the season of the missel-thrush . . . when there is no gleam of light anywhere and no change in that darkness of immense ever-moving cloud above; and the south-west raves all day and all night, and day after day, then the storm-cock sings his loudest from a tree-top and has no rival. A glorious bird! . . . You must believe that this dark aspect of things delights him; that his pleasure in life, expressed with such sounds and in such circumstances, must greatly exceed in degree the contentment and bliss that is ours, even when we are most free from pain and care, and our whole beings most perfectly in tune with nature. . . . The sound is beautiful in quality, but the singer has no art, and flings out his notes anyhow; the song is an outburst, a cry of happiness.

*Darkling:* shrouded in darkness, or taking place in dark-ness. It is a famous poetic word, most notably used by Shakespeare (in *King Lear*), Milton, Keats, and Arnold. A few other words and phrases besides *darkling* clearly echo "Ode to a Nightingale," but certainly Hardy was conscious of the last three lines of "Dover Beach": "And we are here as on a darkling plain / Swept by

confused alarms of struggle and flight, / Where igno-
rant armies clash by night."


*The Ruined Maid*

35.6  *spudding up docks:* spading up weeds [dial.]

35.9  *barton:* farmyard [dial.]

35.17  *hag-ridden:* afflicted by nightmare

35.18  *sock:* sulk, sigh audibly [dial.]

35.19  *megrims:* low spirits, headaches [corruption of *migraine*]


*The Respectable Burgher on "the Higher Criticism"*

36  Although Hardy took very seriously what was called
the Higher Criticism (historical and interpretive, along
with the so-called lower criticism, which was textual
and philological) and its refutation of the literal truth
of Scripture, as well as the geological, biological, and
much other scientific evidence against what for cen-
turies had been taken as revealed truth, he is having a
fine time here, sustaining a single rhyme for thirty-six
lines, inventing droll ways of characterizing some of
the most solemn biblical tales, and making jokes at the
expense of both the revisionist critics and the bourgeois
speaker.

36.1  *Reverend Doctors:* probably the so-called Seven against
Christ, a group of liberal clergymen and intellectuals
(including the formidable classical scholar, Benjamin
Jowett), who in *Essays and Reviews*, published in 1860,
had challenged the authenticity of miracles; they
averred that the language of the Bible is often figurative
and that much of the narrative presented as history is
in fact myth. The *Doctors* may include other contem-
porary biblical scholars, such as John William Colenso
and John Robert Seeley.

36.2  *clerks:* clerics

36.13  *Solomon sang the fleshly Fair:* the critics contended that
the Song of Solomon was an erotic poem, or sequence,
which the Church Fathers had tortured into an allegory
of Christ's love for His Church.

36.24  *the Nain widow's only heir:* a dead man restored to life by Jesus

36.26  *Piombo:* Sebastiano del Piombo, early sixteenth-century painter of the Venetian School. *The Raising of Lazarus* is in the National Gallery in London.

36.27  *Sheol:* the shadowy world of the dead in the Hebrew Bible

36.28  *Jael . . . snare:* the story of Jael's murder of Sisera can be found in Judges 4 (and of Peter's cutting off Malchus' ear in John 18:10). All of the other miraculous episodes should be too familiar to require notes.

37.36  *that moderate man Voltaire:* an ironic joke—Voltaire was a rather immoderate rationalist and skeptic.


*In Tenebris I*

38  The title means, In shadows, or in darkness. The Latin epigraph is from the Vulgate Scriptures; the King James Version renders it, "My heart is smitten, and withered like grass." "Unhope" is a typical Hardyesque coinage (cf. "unbloom" in "Hap"). Its meaning is rather different from that of "hopelessness"—the latter suggests weakness and helplessness and strikes perhaps a note of self-pity; whereas "unhope" bespeaks a simultaneous refusal and acceptance and has in it a kind of unflinching resignation, an almost serene despair.


*A Trampwoman's Tragedy*

41  The ballad is based on a local incident that took place in 1827. Hardy wrote to Edmund Gosse, "The circumstances have been known to me for many years. You may like to be told that the woman's name was Mary Ann Taylor—though she has been dust for half a century." Part of Hardy's note on the poem says of Blue Jimmy that he

> was a notorious horse-stealer of Wessex in those days, who appropriated more than a hundred horses before he was caught, among others one belonging to a neighbour of the

> writer's grandfather. He was hanged at the now
> demolished Ivel-chester or Ilchester jail. . . .

41.15  *landskip:* landscape [dial.]

42.31  *tap:* valve and spout for drawing ale or beer from a
keg; here, a synechdoche for tavern

43.49  *settle:* long bench with arms and back high enough that
one could sit "inside" it
Hardy thought this his most successful poem. In any
case, it was one of his most popular, and certainly it
has more of the flavor of authentic folk balladry than
most such literary imitations.

### The Rejected Member's Wife

46     Colonel William Ernest Brymer had been a Conser-
vative Member of Parliament for Dorchester and then
for South Dorset for over thirty years, until he was
defeated in 1906 by the Liberal candidate. Hardy (who
voted Liberal when he voted) knew and liked Mrs.
Brymer.

### Shut Out That Moon

47     In Dorset lore and in Hardy's poetry, the moon, es-
pecially when seen through glass, is a bad omen. In
Hardy, it is often symbolic of seeing life with cold
clarity—cf. "The Moon Looks In" and "To the
Moon."

47.8   *Lady's Chair:* Cassiopeia

### The Division

48.2   *besom:* sweep with force [dial.] A besom is a broom
made of twigs.

48.9   *thwart:* obstinate; crosswise; adverse [literary]

### After the Club-Dance

52.1   *Black'on:* Black Down, a hill a few miles from Dor-
chester

52.1   *Maidon:* Mai Dun (now known as Maiden Castle), an
ancient hill-fort just outside of Dorchester

### The Market-Girl

52.1 *causey:* causeway; paved or cobbled lane or street [dial.]

### The Inquiry

53.4 *sengreens:* houseleeks; a variety of stonecrop or saxifrage [dial.]

53.7 *hurdled:* built or enclosed with hurdles. Hurdles are temporary fences made of intertwined branches of hazel or willow, used for penning sheep—see "A Sheep Fair."

53.15 *fag:* wearisome work

### After the Fair

54.9 *drongs:* narrow lanes between hedgerows enclosing fields [dial.]

55.20 *burghees:* townsmen, citizens [dial.]

### To Carrey Clavel

55.6 *Dewbeating:* walking vigorously

55.11 *coll:* embrace [dial.]

### The Orphaned Old Maid

56.4 *Make a spouse in your pocket:* F. B. Pinion, author of *A Hardy Companion*, suggests that the girl is being told to save her money by staying single, and he may be right. But I cannot help wondering where a poor country girl would get such money and whether the phrase might not be an earthy local saying, meaning that she can do for herself whatever a husband would do.

### The Homecoming

57 Toller Down is a ridge about fifteen miles northwest of Dorchester; more than one writer has attested to the accuracy of this description of Toller Down in autumn or winter. The young girl is very likely not used either to the weather or to her husband's dialect. If the reader is not used to the meter, it is dipodic, as in many nursery rhymes, like "**BAA** ʙᴀᴀ **BLACK** ꜱʜᴇᴇᴘ / **HAVE** you ᴀɴʏ **WOOL**"—a dipod is a double foot consist-

ing of a strong beat and a weak one, the number of syllables varying, e.g., "And **LONE**some **WAS** the **HOUSE** and **DARK**; and **FEW CAME THERE**." See "His Visitor" and "The Last Signal," which are also dipodic. (Most of "Friends Beyond" is in trochaic octameter and "Wessex Heights" is in loose fourteeners, but lines of that length, especially fourteeners, tend toward the dipodic.)

57.4  *skimmer-cake:* pudding made from leftovers and baked on a metal skimming ladle

57.5  *summat strong:* the something is probably cider [dial.]

57.9  *poppet:* term of endearment: doll, darling [dial.]

59.48  *sock:* sulk, sigh audibly [dial.]

As with "The Ruined Maid" and a number of other poems, the rough humor arises from the treatment of material that, viewed from a slightly different angle, would readily seem pathetic or frightening. Philip Larkin speaks of "an undercurrent of sensual cruelty in the writing— this seems an extraordinary thing to say of Hardy, but for all his gentleness he had a strong awareness of, and even relish for, both the macabre and the cruel."

*A Church Romance*

59  Hardy's mother had told him about her seeing his father for the first time, around 1835. The choir was the string band up in the balcony that projected from the west wall of the church, a band consisting of Hardy's father, grandfather, uncle, and one of their friends. Hardy was a good fiddler by the age of eight; by that time the choir had been disbanded, but a few years later the boy would be playing with his father at weddings and other local merry-makings.

60.14  "*New Sabbath*" or "*Mount Ephraim*": melodies from the Anglican Hymnal (to which hymns or Tate and Brady's metrical psalms were set)

*After the Last Breath*

60  J. H. is Jemima Hardy, the poet's mother, who after a vigorous old age died at the age of ninety-one. The

others present are probably his brother Henry and his two sisters, Mary and Kate. The abrupt enjambment between lines 15 and 16 is a powerfully moving surprise: at the end of line 15, our first thought is likely to be that the cell in which the prisoner is confined is the coffin; but no, the coffin is freedom.

### One We Knew

61 M. H. is Mary Head Hardy, his paternal grandmother, who lived with the family until Hardy was almost seventeen.

61.4 *cots:* cottages [poetical]

61.4 *dip:* candle made of a wick dipped in tallow, as opposed to the fancy wax candles in the panelled mansions

61.5 *"poussetting"* and *"allemanding":* a country dance and any one of various German dances

61.24 *cart-tail:* Only a few decades before Hardy's birth, delinquent children were still being tied to carts and whipped.

### She Hears the Storm

62 The Hardy cottage is the setting for this poem. It is partly surrounded by Thorncombe Wood, and the Frome River is less than a mile to the south.

62.16 *garden-hatch:* small gate or wicket [dial.]

### The Man He Killed

63.4 *nipperkin:* half pint [rare]

63.15 *traps:* gear, belongings

63.20 *half a crown:* a generous loan, worth several dollars at the time of the Boer War

### Channel Firing

69 Hardy would certainly have heard the roar of the guns from English battleships in the spring of 1914: Dorchester is only seven miles north of the coast. Each of the monuments named in the last stanza moves progressively farther back in time and space. Stourton

Tower commemorates the great victory of the Saxon King Alfred over the invading Danes in 879 and praises him for the establishment of the monarchy, the navy, trial by jury, liberty, and other things. Camelot is sometimes imagined to be the citadel of the much earlier and legendary King Arthur, who is supposed to have led the Britons against the Saxons. Stonehenge is the famous prehistoric monument on Salisbury Plain. It is something of a hyperbole to extend the sound of the guns to these ancient sacred places—Stonehenge is some fifty miles away. (Ransom has rightly called attention to the beauty of the stresses on the metrically unaccented second syllables of the last two words— "stárLIT StóneHENGE.") If the poem was prophetic of the outbreak of war three or four months later, it was accidentally so: Hardy, as he said then, had not expected it to come so soon.

69.9 *glebe cow:* a parson's cow

### The Convergence of the Twain

70 This poem, commemorating the sinking of the *Titanic* on April 15, 1912, was completed on April 24; it first appeared in the program of a benefit performance at Covent Garden on May 14 to raise money for the victims of the disaster, and then, with an added stanza (the fifth), in the *Fortnightly Review* on June 1. As almost everyone knows, the "unsinkable" luxury ship on her maiden voyage to New York struck an iceberg and went down in the North Atlantic; more than 1,500 people drowned or froze to death. Hardy had been acquainted with two of the passengers who died.

70.5 *salamandrine:* The salamander was a mythical lizard able to live in fire, which it could extinguish with the low temperature of its own body.

70.6 *thrid:* wind through the labyrinthine passages of [arch.]

72.30 *anon:* before long, sooner or later (in this case) [arch.] The word can have related but different meanings, like "again, at another time" (cf. "The Going") or "at once" (cf. "The Contretemps").

*Wessex Heights*

73  The date of this poem, 1896, is of some importance. The last few years of the century were probably the darkest of Hardy's life. He had suffered from the controversy surrounding *Tess of the D'Urbervilles*; the outcry over *Jude the Obscure* and the brutality of some of the reviews were even worse. His father had died in 1892. His marriage, always difficult, was at its nadir; Emma had even tried to prevent the publication of *Jude*. And there were other sorrows; see "In Tenebris I," written about the same time.

73.6  *Her who suffereth long:* First Corinthians 13:4 (cf. "The Blinded Bird").

*The Schreckhorn*

75  The Schreckhorn is a peak in the Swiss Alps, over 13,000 feet high. Leslie Stephen climbed it in 1861— the first man to do so. He was editor of the *Cornhill Magazine* and published some of Hardy's work, including the serialization of *Far from the Madding Crowd*, one of Hardy's best novels and a popular success. Although he rejected *The Return of the Native* (knowing it would shock his subscribers), he and Hardy remained good friends. Virginia Woolf, Stephen's daughter, told Hardy she regarded this sonnet "as incomparably the truest & most imaginative portrait of him."

*POEMS OF 1912–13*

79  Despite the many years of estrangement and misery, Hardy was devastated by Emma's sudden death in November of 1912. Overwhelmed by immense regret over what their life together had come to and by memories of their early happiness, especially their courting days in Cornwall, he made the long journey to Cornwall in March 1913, an arduous undertaking for a man of seventy-three, and tramped around in the mud and cold of St. Juliot and the cliffs along the coast, seeking out their old trysting places. (See "After a Journey" and "At Castle Boterel.") Hardy regarded these poems as

an "expiation." In the aftermath of Emma's death, he wrote to a friend that he had composed them "when I felt miserable lest I had not treated her considerately in her latter life. However, I shall publish them as the only amends I can make." The twenty-one poems in this sequence are among the most beautiful and most original elegies in the language, but some of them are better than others; I have chosen the eleven that I think the best, beginning with the opening poem, "The Going," and ending with "At Castle Boterel," the sixteenth and perhaps the finest poem in the sequence. He wrote close to a hundred more poems about Emma, lyrics of recollection and self-reproach and mourning, and at least twenty of them are to be found in this book, including "At the Word 'Farewell,'" "Near Lanivet, 1872," "My Spirit Will Not Haunt the Mound," "The Shadow on the Stone," "He Prefers Her Earthly," "Fetching Her," "A Leaving," and "The Marble Tablet." Something of her and of his feelings for her can be found in many other poems.

79  *Veteris vestigia flammae:* traces of an old flame [*Æneid* IV, 23]

### Rain on a Grave

82.2  *amain:* forcefully, in great quantity [arch.]

83.19–36  Emma loved daisies extravagantly, from childhood on. The third stanza breaks off the easy irony of the first half of the poem; the fourth makes unexpected use of it—the cold indifferent pelting rain that once harried her to shelter is what now nourishes the flowers she loved so dearly and will soon be part of.

### Lament

85.28  *Candlemas-time:* around February 2 (when candles are blessed to celebrate the Purification of the Virgin Mary)

### The Haunter

85  This is one of Hardy's greatest poems, better even than its much more anthologized companion poem, "The

Voice" (which echoes the triple rhyme in line 21). The language is utterly simple and lucid; the dramatic moment is strange and complex. The ghost that speaks is a creation of the poet, who is quite oblivious of the presence of his creation, cannot see her or hear her, even as he is setting down her words, words that say that she cannot answer them, which in one sense is literally the case and in another is contradicted by the poem, which is her attempt to answer. The interweaving perspectives of irony are dizzying. And then, what richness and delicacy of tone in the opening of the last stanza—"What a good haunter I am" always summons up for me the echo of Little Jack Horner (his name is even an assonantal rhyme) and raises a smile, but the inflection is also plangent and yearning, the imperative is urgent. "O tell him!"—to whom is she speaking? Not to us—what reader could tell him? The only one who can tell him is the poem; it is the poem she is beseeching.

### The Voice

87.11 *wistlessness:* obliviousness, unknowingness [poetical]—
the Anglo-Saxon root is *wis,* know. (There is also some sense of the opposite of *wistfulness*—death as both absence of knowing and surcease of yearning.)
The dactyllic tetrameter is identical to the measure of a favorite tune from the family songbook, "Haste to the Wedding," though the tune is up-tempo and joyful. If someone suggested that I compose an elegy in this meter, I would think he was mad—almost any poet would. But Hardy seems not to see any difficulty, and he carries it off. The meter changes in the last stanza—a rare thing in Hardy; it shifts down, so to speak, to trochees, a cognate meter; and the penultimate line echoes the tetrameter of the earlier stanzas. The almost inaudible accent on "And" in the last line is thrilling—we hear the line as if it had only two beats, and that seems to distance and elongate the call.

*After a Journey*

89.29  *lours:* appears dark and threatening [variant of *lowers*]

89  *Pentargan Bay:* a small bay on the Cornish coast, circled by steep cliffs; it is less than a mile north of Boscastle.


*"She Charged Me"*

91.11  *curiously:* Like its Latin etymon, *curious* means not only interested, eager to know, but also unduly inquisitive and prying.

I have included this heartsick and unusually acerbic poem because it is strong enough to survive its one clumsy line, "A folly flown ere her reign had place." I have omitted a fair number of poems which I like, because they contain a few too many weak lines or passages. "A Conversation at Dawn," which Pound admired, is a good example: it is a poem of considerable interest and power despite its element of melodrama, but the dialogue is full of stilted, ponderous locutions.


*In the Days of Crinoline*

92  Crinolines were the hooped petticoats and skirts of an earlier time.

92.1  *tilt-bonnet:* bonnet of plain coarse cloth, with wide brim and wings half-hiding the face

93.19  *severally:* separately

93.24  *conned:* peered at, scrutinized [arch.]


*Exeunt Omnes*

95  The title is a familiar old stage-direction, meaning "Everyone goes out." The manuscript is dated June 2, 1913, Hardy's seventy-third birthday and barely half a year after Emma's death.

95.10  *Kennels:* gutters, street drains


## SATIRES OF CIRCUMSTANCE IN FIFTEEN GLIMPSES

96  Hardy wrote to a friend in 1911, "You will remember, I am sure, that being *satires* they are rather brutal. I

express no feeling or opinion myself at all." He wrote later that they were "caustically humorous productions which had been issued with a light heart before the war," and that he would have suppressed them, had they not become so well known from publication in magazines and anthologies. (Two or three are based on true stories.) Here is Ransom's useful and delightful account of the nature of these often underrated poems:

> They must be taken in the comic sense which is intended. They are satires rather than proper tragedies, being poems in which the victims are not entitled to our sympathy. The joke is upon persons who have to be punished because they were foolish; because they were more innocent than anybody can afford to be in this world. The qualified reader is one who is able as he reads to recover his sophistication quickly if he had the least inclination to be sympathetic. Hardy means to try the propriety of our responses. And this time there are no Subalterns to execute the sentence in obedience to Heaven; but members of the victims' own kind, with cruelties and treacheries peculiarly human, and made possible because the victims have exposed themselves where they were most vulnerable, being infatuated or vain and self-righteous. The Satires represent Hardy about mid-point of his poetic career in a mood of ferocity which we might hardly have expected. He enlarges himself for us in respect of his psychic capabilities, though the gentle reader may not like him any the better.

*In the Room of the Bride-Elect*
97.4 *mollyish*: timid, wimpy [dial.]

*Over the Coffin*

103.13  *parochial:* provincial, narrow-minded

*"We Sat at the Window"*

107  Bournemouth is a coastal resort about twenty miles east of Weymouth. St. Swithin's Day falls on July 15 (and according to folklore, rain on that day presages another forty days of rain). Hardy and Emma had been married a little less than a year.

*At the Word "Farewell"*

108  Hardy, writing to Edmund Gosse in 1918, said of his poems, "I myself (naturally I suppose) like those best which are literally true," and named two poems as examples, of which this was one. It describes the early dawn of March 11, 1870, as Hardy was preparing to leave St. Juliot, having made his measurements, drawings, and estimates for the restoration of the church, and having made the acquaintance of Emma Lavinia Gifford—an encounter that would prove to be the central event of his life.

108.11  *As of chances the chance furthermost:* the slimmest of all chances

*Heredity*

109.4  *times anon:* times to come

*Near Lanivet, 1872*

109  This was the other poem Hardy named as being "literally true." He and Emma had gone to Bodmin to see her father, to speak to him about their engagement. It was not a successful visit. John Gifford, writes Michael Millgate (Hardy's best biographer), "greeted his prospective son-in-law with open contempt" and later referred to Hardy as "the low-born churl who has presumed to marry into *my* family." Mr. Gifford, although better born, was a disbarred solicitor and a drunk.

109.1  *stunted handpost:* in reality, a stone marker with a Greek cross carved on its face—perhaps in 1872 there was a handpost there, but the carved cross would have been enough for the drama of the poem.

### Timing Her

112 Lalage was the name of the fifteen-year-old daughter of the curator of the Dorset County Museum, a friend of Hardy's, who sometimes sent her to Max Gate with a message. It is certainly not to be imagined that Hardy was planning an assignation with this young girl; Lalage, as Hardy well knew, is also the name of a girl celebrated in Horace's Ode I, 22—*dulce ridentem Lalagen amabo / dulce loquentem*—and II, 5. This erotic daydream is altogether literary (though real enough to the poet, with its rapid, insistent dimeters and repetitions).

113.38 *vair:* The slippers are lined with white or grey squirrel fur.

113.51 *Fain I'd avow:* I would readily confess.

### The Blinded Bird

114 It was long known that this cruel operation would induce automatic song. The last stanza is a paraphrase of First Corinthians 13:4–7. Of all the things that outraged Hardy, the one that most raised his gorge was cruelty to animals. "He strove that such innocent creatures should come to no harm, / But he could do little for them; and now he is gone."

### To My Father's Violin

116 Hardy's grandfather played bass-viol (viola da gamba, an early cello) in the choir—that is, the string band—of Stinsford Church (a choir he himself established), twice every Sunday from 1801 until his death in 1837; in his later years he was joined by his sons and friends. By the time Hardy was old enough to join *his* father, the choir had been disbanded, but later he and his father played at many local festivities. Hardy kept his father's old violin in his study for the thirty-five years that he survived him; it can be seen in the reconstructed study now in the Dorset County Museum, and

can be heard on recordings (see the note to "In the Small Hours"). This poem was harshly criticized for its pagan references and its deep sadness. Hardy wrote to a friend, ". . . I have had sent me a review which quotes a poem entitled 'To My Father's Violin,' containing a Virgilian reminiscence of mine of Acheron and the Shades. The writer comments: 'Truly this pessimism is insupportable. . . . One marvels that Hardy is not in a madhouse.' Such is English criticism, and I repeat, why did I ever write a line!"

116.2   *Nether Glooms:* like *Mournful Meads* in the fourth stanza, a Hardyism for the underworld, which here somewhat resembles Sheol, or Hades (of which Acheron is one of the five rivers)

116.14   *quire:* quoir (string band) [dial.] (See "A Church Romance.")

116.18   *eff-holes:* the f-shaped apertures in violins

117.43   *Purflings:* inlaid ivory or mother-of-pearl ornamenting the edges of a violin [arch.]

117.44   *con:* study, ponder [arch.]


*The Pedigree*

117.6   *green-rheumed:* This is a very odd usage. It must mean that the clouds are full of moisture, as if flowing with mucous, or tears, and it leads into the astonishing image of the dolphin's eye.

118.13   *Mage:* magician

118.23–26   *That every heave . . . by their so making it:* That everything I thought or felt or said was shown in the mirror to have been long ago anticipated by their will and their acts

118.27   *fuglemen:* leaders, exemplars; a fugleman is an expert soldier who demonstrates the drill to recruits

Hardy was fascinated by genealogy all his life. He believed that the Hardys (like the D'Urbervilles) were a once distinguished family that had come down in the world, and he took great pride in being a descendant, as he thought, of the Thomas Hardy who was Nelson's flag-captain at Trafalgar, in whose arms Nelson died.

(Nelson's last words are supposed to have been, "Kiss me, Hardy." A few jocular scholars have suggested that he said, "Kismet, Hardy.")

### Where They Lived

119.4 *bents:* a kind of grass with stiff stalks

### "Something Tapped"

120.11 *pallid moth:* The white miller moth was believed to be the soul of a dead person. (See "Friends Beyond" and "Afterwards.") J. O. Bailey, author of the very useful *The Poetry of Thomas Hardy: A Handbook and Commentary*, adds that a tapping on the pane would be taken as an omen of death.

### The Oxen

121.13 *barton:* farmyard [dial.]

121.13 *coomb:* glen or narrow valley [dial.]
Cf. *Tess of the D'Urbervilles*, Chapter XVII, where Hardy makes use of the same folk belief.

### An Anniversary

122.6 *stile:* set of steps to allow people to go over a hedge or fence

122.12 *pedlar:* peddler

122.16 *garth:* enclosed grounds, in this case the Stinsford churchyard [dial.]

### Transformations

123 In this little vision of the afterlife, the dead ascend to the *upper air*, almost resurrected in the flesh—their nerves and veins are now the branches of trees and the veins of leaves. Everything is transformed—grandsire to nursling, red to green, flesh to grass, a girl to a rose, and all the old-fashioned and biblical words to *energy*. The four elements have their part. Even the sounds participate—the lightness of line 12 with its barely audible middle accent seems to modulate perfectly the delicacy of the girl's slipping into love's flower; and the

nasals (the key, as it were, that the poem is written in)—there is at least one in every line, very often there are three. Other consonants recur: *grandsire, green, grasses, underground, growths.* A poem of ninety-five words, seventy-eight of them monosyllabic. (Eugenio Montale, who translated some of Hardy's poems, wrote, perhaps a little glumly, that "the intricate net that Hardy cast to encompass his poetry demands a saturation of monosyllables such as can be found only in the English language.")

*The Last Signal*

123 William Barnes kept a school in Dorchester, next to the office where young Hardy was employed as an apprentice architect; he and the old man became friends. Barnes was for the most part self-educated, a philologist and clergyman who knew a score of languages, and a fine poet, who wrote in dialect. He had a strong influence on his young friend, an influence most visible in many of Hardy's coinages—for instance, *fellow-yearsmen* for "contemporaries" ("His Immortality") and *foot-folk* for "pedestrians" ("The Five Students"). Barnes thought that English had become too Latinate and advocated the substitution of words with Anglo-Saxon roots. This argument had recurred more than once since the "inkhorn" controversy of the sixteenth century, and Barnes was not alone in his conviction. Gerard Manley Hopkins and W. W. Skeat were two of many dedicated to writing and fostering a purer English. Hopkins, although he did think Barnes' program hopelessly extreme, was sympathetic. He wrote to Bridges in 1882,

> It makes one weep to think what English might have been; for in spite of all that Shakspere and Milton have done with the compound I cannot doubt that no beauty in a language can make up for lack of purity. In fact I am learning Anglosaxon and it is a vastly superior thing to what we have now.

Hopkins' own language is often as close to Anglo-Saxon as modern English can well be, and many of his coinages are not very different from Hardy's—*before-time-taken, yestertempest, anvil-ding, forepang, undenizened, bone-house, wanwood,* and so on.)

If you walked down Winterborne Came Path and followed it up to the crest of the long hill opposite Hardy's house at Max Gate, you would see, down among the trees, the roof of the rectory where the Reverend Barnes lived and the road on which Hardy saw his coffin being borne to the graveyard. As an additional act of piety, Hardy is imitating here a Welsh form that William Barnes was fond of and sometimes used in his own work. It requires an intricate pattern of consonants (called *cynghanedd*) and an internal rhyme in the second line of each quatrain (called *union*). The meter is dipodic.

### At Middle-Field Gate in February

125 Middle-Field refers to the fields around the Hardy cottage in Higher Bockhampton, and the "bevy now underground" were the young field-women Hardy knew as a boy, some of whose names he could remember in old age—Unity Sargent, Eliza Trevis, Ann West, Susan Chamberlain, Elizabeth Hurden, Esther Oliver, Anna Barrett, Emma Shipton, and others.

### On Sturminster Foot-Bridge

126.4 *scrabbled:* scribbled, marked randomly
126.8 *eyot-withies:* willows or other pliant shoots on a little island

### Old Furniture

127.22 *whilom:* formerly [lit.]
127.22 *the nut:* the fixed ridge on the neck of a violin over which the strings pass
127.28 *linten:* made of cotton wool or other fluffy material [coinage]. Fires were made by igniting these bits of fluff with a flint and steel.

*Logs on the Hearth*

128  Mary, the sister Hardy was closest to, died in November 1915.

*The Ballet*

130.9  *muster:* come together, appear (This is a good example of an odd or quaint word that on reflection comes to seem the best possible word.)

*The Five Students*

130  The five "students" (or at least four of them) can be identified with reasonable certainty: *dark He* is probably Horace Moule, Hardy's dearest friend in his youth, who died early, by his own hand; *dark She* may be Hardy's cousin, Tryphena Sparks, with whom he is thought to have had an affair; *fair She* is Emma. It is interesting and enriching to recognize the actual people who have taken on another life in Hardy's poems; it should go without saying that their identities are not essential to understanding and enjoying the poems.

131.25  *tag the church-aisle leads:* hang from the strips of lead between the panes of a latticed or stained-glass window

*At a Country Fair*

134  Based on a newspaper item. Hardy wrote in one of his notebooks, "Blind Giant.—His dimensions had attracted cupidity of an exhibitor, who had barely allowed him necessaries and kept him a sort of prisoner. Age 19." Although an excellent poem and relatively pure in diction, it almost never appears in the anthologies or selections.

*Jubilate*

135  The title means "Make a joyful noise."

135.7  *the great breastplate:* Exodus 28:15

135.8  *Urim and Thummim:* sacred objects used for divination, to find out the will of God. God gives Moses elaborate instructions for making the ceremonial garments that

Aaron will wear as High Priest; after explaining how
the breastplate is to be studded with twelve precious
stones representing the tribes of Israel, God tells Moses,
"And thou shalt put in the breastplate of judgment the
Urim and the Thummim; and they shall be upon the
heart of Aaron, when he goeth in before the Lord."
The nature of these lots is unknown; even the origin
of the names can only be guessed at.

135.13 *hautboys, and shawms:* oboes, and early wind instru-
ments similar to oboes

135.21 *chore:* quoir, or chorus [dial.]

135.22 *Little-Ease:* life [a prison cell too small to stand up or
lie down in; specifically, the name of one of the dun-
geons in the Tower of London]

### Midnight on the Great Western

136 The description is very similar to that of Little Father
Time, the boy in *Jude the Obscure*.

### The Shadow on the Stone

137 The "Druid stone," as Hardy called it, was a five-foot
stone that had been discovered three feet underground,
covered with ashes and charred bones. It took seven
men to dig it out and erect it on the lawn at Max Gate,
where it stands to this day. It may have been an ancient
menhir; in any case, Hardy regarded it with awe. (The
poem echoes the story of Orpheus and Euridyce.)

### In the Garden

138 M. H. is Mary Hardy (see "Logs on the Hearth").

### The Choirmaster's Burial

139 This is an imaginative retelling of the story of Hardy's
grandfather's burial. The *lutes* are figurative: the choir
played violins and cellos.

139.13 *"Mount Ephraim":* name of a melody from the
hymnal—see "A Church Romance."

140.47 *the tenor man* (tenor violin): Hardy's father

### In Time of "The Breaking of Nations"

141  Of this Hardy wrote, "the poem . . . contains a feeling
     that moved me in 1870, during the Franco-Prussian
     War, when I chanced to be looking at such an agri-
     cultural incident in Cornwall. But I did not write the
     verses till during the war with Germany of 1914. . . ."
     The phrase "The breaking of nations" comes from Jer-
     emiah 51:20—God's judgment against Babylon.

141.6  *couch-grass:* tough weeds which are dug up and burned
       in piles

141.9  *wight:* living creature (in this case a man) [arch.]

### Afterwards

142.1  *postern:* back gate of a garden [rare]

142.6  *dewfall-hawk:* not the name of the hawk but an epithet
       which, like the eyelid's blink, figures the alighting of the
       hawk. (A couple of editors have confidently identified
       this creature as a moth, but that cannot possibly be right.
       Would any competent poet write of a moth that it
       "comes crossing the shades to alight / Upon the wind-
       warped upland thorn"? In any case, James Gibson has
       identified it as the nightjar, and that settles it.) As for
       comparing the approach of the hawk to an eyelid's
       soundless blink, is there a better simile in English poetry?

142.17 *quittance:* The word strongly suggests leaving or ceasing;
       in fact, it means release, or discharge of a debt, or the ful-
       filling of an obligation, or recompense, or reprisal. [arch.]

142.18 The sound of *outrollings* is choice, the pronunciation
       slightly distorted by the meter and rhyme, which re-
       quires an accent on the final syllable.

### "According to the Mighty Working"

146  Hardy wrote of this poem, "In February he [Hardy]
     signed a declaration of sympathy with the Jews in sup-
     port of a movement for 'the reconstitution of Palestine
     as a National Home for the Jewish people'. . . . about
     the same time there appeared a relevant poem by
     Hardy in *The Atheneum* . . . entitled in words from the
     Burial Service." (The reason that Hardy is speaking of

himself in the third person is that he wrote or dictated two volumes of autobiography that were published after his death under the name of his second wife, Florence Emily Dugdale, and were meant to be taken as her work. What could be more fitting than that Hardy should be the ghost of his own biography?) The poem was written after the end of the Great War, and it is clear that Hardy thought of *Peace, this hid riot, Change*, as referring, at least in part, to the agitation against the British mandate over Palestine. This beautiful little poem should give pause to those who believe that all poems must contain imagery and physical details: except for a few words and phrases, like "the dusk" and the "spinner's wheel," its diction is almost entirely abstract. Even the concrete words are rather abstract.

146.1 *moiling:* drudgery; vexation; milling about in confusion

### The Contretemps

148 The action of this poem is set in Weymouth on the same bridge where the sailor meets his wife in "The Harbour Bridge." An oddly touching poem, in spite of its melodramatic plot and the troubling question of what happened to the woman whom the speaker was originally awaiting.

148.13 *anon:* (in this context) at once, or very soon

149.46 *pother:* mental distress, turmoil [dial.]

### The Fallow Deer at the Lonely House

150 The fallow deer is a Mediterranean deer, smaller than the red deer and of a pale brownish or yellowish color.

150.6 *fender-brink:* the edge of the metal frame fitted to a fireplace to keep coals from rolling out

150.12 The last line is particularly beautiful, with its hovering between meter and pronunciation, much like the last two words of "Channel Firing."

### On the Tune Called the Old-Hundred-and-Fourth

151 This is a setting from *The Whole Book of Psalms*, published in 1621 and often reprinted, the best known work of a seventeenth-century musician, Thomas Ravenscroft.

151.15  *Sheol:* Hebrew abode of the dead (See "The Respect-
able Burgher"—neither Lazarus nor anyone else can
return from Sheol.)

### Voices from Things Growing in a Churchyard

152  All of the deceased are actual people whose graves can
still be seen in Stinsford Churchyard. Walking there
with Walter de la Mare, Hardy pointed out the head-
stones and memorial tablets. "Fanny Hurd's real name
was Fanny Hurden, and Hardy remembered her as a
delicate child who went to school with him. She died
when she was about eighteen. . . . The others men-
tioned in this poem were known to him by name and
repute." The headstone above Thomas Voss's grave is
near Hardy's grave; Grey and Bowring are commem-
orated on tablets in the church; Hardy had read the
story of Eve Trevelyan in the parish register (she was
the mother of two or three illegitimate children).

153.33  *withwind:* a clematis called "the virgin's bower" [Har-
dy's note]

153.35  *Greensleeves:* as in the popular Elizabethan ballad, an
easy woman: presumably her sleeves have been stained
by lying too often on the grass.

### A Two-Years' Idyll

154  This deeply sad poem recalls the two years (1876 to
1878) that he and Emma lived in Sturminster Newton,
a period that Hardy later thought of as "our happiest
time."

### Fetching Her

155  This is clearly about having taken Emma out of her
native Cornwall and the keen regret that her life in
Dorset had not brought her much happiness; but some
of the details are freely invented.

155.17  *mews:* seagulls

155.19  *expugn:* assault, overwhelm

A Procession of Dead Days

156   Another poem about life with Emma, beginning with their first meeting in the dusk at St. Juliot, including their courtship, engagement, and nuptials, the difficult years of marriage, and ending with her death. This poem is beyond praise.

156.6   *anon:* (as the repetition suggests) again, but it could easily carry its other senses—come soon, come at once, etc.

156.23   *rainbow sign:* the sign of God's covenant with Noah after the flood

156.29   *queue:* tail—a trope for the wake of the meteor

157.41–42   *When his original glossed the thrums / Of ivy:* when the original day illuminated, or made glossy, the multitude of ivy leaves. (The word *thrums* in this sense is archaic and very rare, apparently not in use for four or five centuries. It seems summoned chiefly for the rhyme; nevertheless, it is a beautiful stanza, the last two lines particularly expressive.)

157.48   *third hour:* that is to say, the third hour after dawn. Emma died at around 9 A.M. And Hardy would certainly have had Mark 15:25 in mind: "It was the third hour, and they crucified him." See "Near Lanivet, 1872."

In the Small Hours

157   Hardy in his boyhood was an excellent fiddler and, with his father, played jigs, reels, and hornpipes by the hour at harvest suppers, weddings, christenings, New Year's Eve revels, and the like. (There is a superb recording of many of these tunes from the handwritten family songbook, called "The Musical Heritage of Thomas Hardy" [Academy Sound and Vision Ltd.]. The Yetties, young musicians from Dorset, play a great number of them [including "Haste to the Wedding," "The New-Rigged Ship," "The Triumph," and so on] on Hardy's own violin and on his father's, borrowed from the Dorset County Museum and renovated for the occasion.)

157.9  *soon anon:* soon afterward

158.20  *amain:* with great force [arch.]

### The Dream Is—Which?

158.13  *heys:* [variant of *hays*] country dances with interweaving steps

### Lonely Days

159   The first stanza seems to deal with Emma's life at Max Gate, the second with her years in St. Juliot, and the third with her visit to Plymouth for her father's funeral (Plymouth had been her girlhood home). Part of the effect, I think, lies in the second stanza's being twice the length of the first and the third's being almost twice the length of the second. (And is there another poet who has written so much and so well in dimeters, whether strict as in "To Lizbie Browne" or loose as in this one?)

### The Marble Tablet

160   Hardy designed a memorial tablet for Emma, and visited St. Juliot in September of 1916 to make sure that it had been erected. Later a tablet for him was set next to it.

161.6  *November:* Emma was born on November 24, 1840, and died on November 27, 1912.

### The Master and the Leaves

161.12  *nightjar:* the nighthawk, which appears at dusk to feed on insects. It makes a distinctive churring sound. (See "Afterwards" and "A Hurried Meeting.")

161.12  *treen:* trees [arch. and lit.]

### Last Words to a Dumb Friend

162   This could be one of several cats. Both Hardy and his wife loved animals and gave their pets the run of the house, often to the dismay of guests. At the edge of the garden at Max Gate there are a dozen or so stones marking the graves of various cats and dogs. The first half of the poem is perhaps not especially distinguished,

but it rises to great dignity and power in the last
twenty-five or thirty lines.

*An Ancient to Ancients*

164.6  *tabrets:* little drums

164.11–12  *God wot / Their fancy:* God knows what their whims
might have been. (The language is as old-fashioned as
the tabrets.)

165.24  *schottische:* a Scottish dance something like a polka

165.26–27  *The "Girl" . . . And "Trovatore":* "The Bohemian
Girl," popular in its day, and the famous Verdi opera
were great favorites of Hardy's.

165.31–34  *Etty . . . Sand:* three genre painters and four novelists,
all of them fashionable and much admired in the mid-
dle of the nineteenth century. Bailey suggests that in-
asmuch as Hardy was not fond of all of them, he may
have been smiling a little at the sentimental tastes of
the age.

165.39  *creeper-nails:* supports for tendrils (See Tennyson's
"Mariana," of which an echo or two has appropriately
found its way into this stanza: "The rusted nails fell
from the knots . . ." etc.)

166.46–47  *our rout / Is imminent to Aïdes' den:* our assemblage of
guests; or, our tumult and noise; or, our headlong flight
is soon to be entering Hades, the land of the dead.

166.54–55  *not alien / From enterprise, to their long last:* like Hardy
himself, not deterred by their great age from doing
their work.

*Waiting Both*

169.7–8  *Wait . . . Till my change come:* Job 14:14
We must know by now how to take such conventions
in Hardy's poetry; he is, after all, a poet who talks to
the moon, to a sea-cliff, to a chrysanthemum, to Time,
as if it were the most natural thing in the world. What
is more surprising is "I and you"—the slightly odd
word order. But of course the star *would* put himself
first: it's a matter of degree; and the introduction of
the idea of degree is what keeps that "I" from being

invidious—after all, the star is immeasurably older and immeasurably larger. Perhaps "degree" suggested itself as a witty way of accounting for the odd word order —I imagine that "mean to do" was thought of first, and dictated the rhyme. And in the astronomical context, "degree" is near to hand. The repetition of "mean to do" does not strike me with any particular force— it is just one of Hardy's familiar repetitions, pleasant enough. But how conclusive and satisfying that repetition is at the very end. Perhaps it was as much a surprise to Hardy as it is to us; sometimes a habitual device suddenly turns out to be a fortunate and handsome stroke.

### A Bird-Scene at a Rural Dwelling
169.6 *codlin-tree:* [variant of *codling*] a kind of apple tree
169.8 *costard:* another kind of apple tree

### Coming Up Oxford Street: Evening
170.11 *chymists:* [*chemists*] pharmacists

### A Sheep Fair
173.5 *hurdles:* temporary fences of intertwined branches of hazel or willow, for confining a group of sheep—*each meek, mewed band.*

### The Calf
174.4 *milcher:* a milk cow
(I have inserted this uncollected poem in *Human Shows.*)

### No Buyers
176.7 *Turk's-head brush:* a long-headed broom
177.21 *in nursing-wise:* cradled in her arms

### One Who Married Above Him
177.3 *night-rime:* nocturnal frost
178.18 *whimmed her:* behaved capriciously, took a sudden fancy
179.39 *Ham-Hill:* a handsome orange-tinted stone quarried not

far from Dorchester. J. O. Bailey notes that this detail
and the mullioned windows suggest a house somewhat
grander than Steve could easily afford.

This poem, especially the second half of it, seems to
me a moving example of what Pound praised in
Hardy—clarity, directness, the attention completely
engaged with the subject, not one inappropriate or
fancy or inveigling word. Nothing for show.

### Nobody Comes

180 The occasion of this poem is Florence's return from
the hospital where she had undergone surgery in Oc-
tober of 1924. Hardy's brother was driving her home,
and they were late. The poem turns out to have little
if anything to do with its occasion. So many of Hardy's
poems grow out of something very simple and often
unpromising; he will take whatever subject offers itself,
however small and homely it might be—like this one:

> They are great trees, no doubt, by now,
> That were so thin in bough—
> That row of limes—
> When we housed there; I'm loth to reckon when;
> The world has turned so many times,
> So many, since then!

In "Nobody Comes," the old man does not conceal
his loneliness, but neither does it seem to be his pur-
pose to present it or relieve it; nor does it in any way
hinder the clarity of his perceptions. For all his aware-
ness of pain and suffering, he is utterly without self-
pity.

### The Harbour Bridge

181 This bridge crosses the River Wey shortly before its
estuary widens into the sea. Although the old bridge
has been replaced, one standing at sundown on the
quay to the east and looking up would see much the

same thing, the people crossing silhouetted against
the bright sky, "as cut black-paper portraits hastening
on." (Silhouette portraiture was very popular in Wey-
mouth in those days.)

181.6   *cutwater:* wedge-shaped end of a bridge pier, dividing
the current

181.9   *painters:* mooring ropes attached to the bows of boats

181.10  *bollards:* the low posts on the quay to which the ropes
are fastened


### Retty's Phases

183     Dated 1868, when Hardy was working in London, this
is the earliest surviving manuscript of a Hardy poem.
*Hot-up scarlet red* is one of those quaint usages we often
smile at, but it is good, vivid English, isn't it? In an
earlier draft, he had written *colour cherry red.*

184.27  *clown:* rustic, peasant

Hardy's note on the poem:

> In many villages it was customary after the fu-
> neral of an unmarried young woman to ring a
> peal as for her wedding while the grave was
> being filled in, as if Death were not to be al-
> lowed to balk her of bridal honours. Young
> unmarried men were always her bearers.


### The Sundial on a Wet Day

184.6   *gnomon:* the style, or triangular plate, that casts a
shadow on a sundial (from the Greek word meaning,
to know)

185.14  *He:* Seen or unseen, the sun is the one consistently
benevolent deity in Hardy's poetry (cf. "Coming Up
Oxford Street: Evening").


### Shortening Days at the Homestead

185.2   *woof-lines:* threads that cross from side to side in a loom,
crossing the warp

185.5   *shock-headed:* shaggy and unkempt

185.6 *pollard:* severely pruned, the branches sometimes taken off
to be used in caning or making hurdles

### A Hurried Meeting
187.52 *imp:* mock like an imp or demon [nonce-use]

### A Leaving
188 The first line and the month should make it clear that
the car is a hearse. Appropriately enough, the end-
words of the first stanza are repeated in reverse order
in the second stanza.

### Proud Songsters
191 Hardy said that he made use of some of his rejected
early poems by prosing them and embedding them in
his novels, and indeed a fair number of passages do bear
strong resemblances to various poems, perhaps none
more than the opening paragraph of Chapter xx in *Tess
of the D'Urbervilles:* "The season developed and ma-
tured. Another year's instalment of flowers, leaves,
nightingales, thrushes, finches, and such ephemeral
creatures, took up their positions where only a year
ago others had stood in their place when these were
nothing more than germs and inorganic particles." In
both stanzas the meter changes from Hardy's charac-
teristic loose line, a mix of iambs and anapests, to strict
iambic. I notice it more clearly in the second stanza.
That breath of eternity that sometimes seems to come
so easily into Hardy's lyrics has something to do with
the slowing down of the movement: the longer caesura
in "No finches were, nor nightingales," the longer
pause after "thrushes"—the same line in the first stanza
is a run-on—and the stately movement of the last two
lines, the last line especially with its clear coincidence
of phrase and foot. (Suppose the last two lines went,
"Nothing but particles of grain, / And the earth, and
air, and the rain." Nearly the same lines—just the syn-
onym for "only" and two extra syllables, the articles in
the last line—but all the power has vanished.) And

where is the fourth element? The sun is just about gone in the very first line and maybe we have forgotten it by now—and this poet is too orderly to make do with only three. The fire comes back in *brand new* (another surprising and Hardyesque word that turns out to be just right)—as the O.E.D. defines it, "as if glowing from the furnace." The *birds* are the fire, the vital element, that lay dormant in the others. I have always thought of this poem as a companion piece to "Transformations," a vision of the beforelife, so to speak.

### Expectation and Experience

192.13 *lew of a wall:* the part of the wall that shelters her from the weather

Another poem, like "Nobody Comes," in which very little happens—one could scarcely call it an incident— yet which in its spare and precise detail, its workmanship and its simple humanity is a good little poem, one that many poets would like to have written.

### Throwing a Tree

193 This poem's first publication was posthumous, in the French journal *Commerce*, under the title "Felling a Tree." (Florence had been asked for one of Hardy's poems and she sent this one, unaware that Hardy had at some point changed the title.) It appeared in the Winter 1928 issue, alongside a translation by Paul Valéry. This fact was startling and interesting enough, and the translation so difficult to find, that I thought some readers would be pleased to have it here. (One might wish that he had done it in rhyming alexandrines; nevertheless, it is a fairly scrupulous trot.)

### ABATAGE D'UN ARBRE

> *D'un pas majestueux les deux exécuteurs s'avancent sur les tertres.*
> *Ils portent deux lourdes haches aux fers larges et brillants, et une longue scie à deux mains, flexible, aux*

*dents faites pour entamer les troncs puissants.*

*Tel ils approchent de l'arbre superbe qui montre sur son flanc la marque de mort.*

*Ils ont mis vestes bas; ils balancent les haches; ils frappent à coups redoublés, juste au ras de la terre.*

*Autour d'eux volent les éclats; de blancs éclats couvrent la mousse et les feuilles tombées.*

*Bientôt une large et profonde entaille tranche 'écorce tout autour du tronc.*

*Et l'un des hommes essaie d'envoyer une corde au haut de l'arbre, et il finit par y parvenir.*

*La scie intervient alors, et travaille jusqu'à ce que la cime du haut géant frissonne. A chaque passage de la lame on voit croître et s'étendre ses frissons.*

*Les hommes retirent la scie; ils pèsent sur le câble. Mais l'arbre ne fait encore que chanceler, et eux s'agenouillent et se remettent à scier. Derechef ils s'écartent, ils essayent encore de tirer l'arbre bas.*

*Enfin le mât vivant s'incline, s'incline plus encore. Avec un cri, Job et Ike se jettent de côté. Parvenu à la fin de sa longue résistance, l'arbre craque et s'abat. Il ébranle en tombant tous les arbres qui l'entourent, et deux cents ans de croissance constante sont anéantis en moins de deux heures.*

### Henley Regatta

194 This regatta is an international rowing competition at Henley-on-Thames, one of the major sporting and social events in England.

### A Forgotten Miniature

196 This locket containing a miniature portrait of Emma in her youth and a lock of her hair was found shortly after her death. I have seen it in the Berg Collection in the New York Public Library.

# INDEX OF TITLES
# AND FIRST LINES

A foreward rush by the lamp in the gloom, 148
A load of brushes and baskets and cradles and chairs, 176
A plain tilt-bonnet on her head, 92
A shaded lamp and a waving blind, 30
A star looks down at me, 169
*"According to the Mighty Working,"* 146
*After a Journey,* 88
*After the Club-Dance,* 52
*After the Fair,* 54
*After the Last Breath,* 60
*Afternoon Service at Mellstock,* 107
*Afterwards,* 142
*"Ah, Are You Digging on My Grave?",* 75
"Ah, are you digging on my grave, 75
Aloof, as if a thing of mood and whim, 75
An hour before the dawn, 155
*Ancient to Ancients, An,* 164
And are ye one of Hermitage—, 53
"And now to God the Father," he ends, 96
*Anniversary, An,* 122
As I drive to the junction of lane and highway, 89
At a bygone Western country fair, 134
*At a Country Fair,* 134
*At a Hasty Wedding,* 28
*At a Watering-Place,* 98
*At Casterbridge Fair,* 51
*At Castle Boterel,* 89
*At Day-Close in November,* 78
*At Middle-Field Gate in February,* 125
*At Tea,* 96

*At the Altar-Rail*, 100
*At the Draper's*, 102
*At the Word "Farewell,"* 108
*August Midnight, An*, 30

*Backward Spring, A*, 133
*Ballad Singer, The*, 51
*Ballet, The*, 129
*Before and After Summer*, 77
*Bird-Scene at a Rural Dwelling, A*, 169
Black'on frowns east on Maidon, 52
*Blinded Bird, The*, 114
Breathe not, hid Heart: cease silently, 22
"But hear. If you stay, and the child be born, 101
*By Her Aunt's Grave*, 97

*Caged Goldfinch, The*, 129
*Calf, The*, 174
*Channel Firing*, 69
*Choirmaster's Burial, The*, 139
Christmas Eve, and twelve of the clock, 120
*Church Romance, A*, 59
Close up the casement, draw the blind, 47
Clouds spout upon her, 82
*Coming Up Oxford Street: Evening*, 170
*Contretemps, The*, 148
*Convergence of the Twain, The*, 70

*Darkling Thrush, The*, 33
Dear Lizbie Browne, 24
Dishevelled leaves creep down, 119
*Division, The*, 48
Does he want you down there, 116
*Domicilium*, 1
*Dream Is—Which?, The*, 158
*Drummer Hodge*, 15
*During Wind and Rain*, 131

*Embarcation*, 15
Every branch big with it, 175

Everybody else, then, going, 95
*Exeunt Omnes*, 95
*Expectation and Experience*, 192

*Fallow Deer at the Lonely House, The*, 150
*Fetching Her*, 155
*Five Students, The*, 130
*Forgotten Miniature, A*, 196
*Former Beauties*, 51
*Friends Beyond*, 7
From here, the quay, one looks above to mark, 181
From Wynyard's Gap the livelong day, 41

*Garden Seat, The*, 145
*"Gentleman's Second-Hand Suit, A,"* 195
*Going and Staying*, 147
*Going, The*, 79
*Great Things*, 124
Gruffly growled the wind on Toller downland broad and bare, 57

"Had he and I but met, 63
*Hap*, 5
*Harbour Bridge, The*, 181
*Haunter, The*, 85
He does not think that I haunt here nightly, 85
He enters, and mute on the edge of a chair, 99
He often would ask us, 139
*He Prefers Her Earthly*, 132
*Henley Regatta*, 194
Here by the moorway you returned, 80
Here is the ancient floor, 37
Here it is hanging in the sun, 195
Here we broached the Christmas barrel, 45
Here, where Vespasian's legions struck the sands, 15
*Heredity*, 109
Hereto I come to view a voiceless ghost, 88
*His Immortality*, 28
*His Visitor*, 87
*Homecoming, The*, 57

*House of Hospitalities, The*, 45
How I was caught, 182
How she would have loved, 84
*Hurried Meeting, A*, 186


I am laughing by the brook with her, 158
I am the family face, 109
*"I Am the One"*, 191
I am the one whom ringdoves see, 191
I bent in the deep of night, 117
I come across from Mellstock while the moon wanes weaker, 87
I drip, drip here, 184
"I had a holiday once," said the woman—, 192
I have risen again, 91
I know not how it may be with others, 126
I lay in my bed and fiddled, 157
I leant upon a coppice gate, 33
*"I Look Into My Glass,"* 11
I look into my glass, 11
I marked when the weather changed, 150
*"I Need Not Go"*, 27
I need not go, 27
I saw a dead man's finer part, 28
I saw it—pink and white—revealed, 128
*"I say I'll Seek Her,"* 48
I say, "I'll seek her side, 48
I see the ghost of a perished day, 156
"I stood at the back of the shop, my dear, 102
I told her when I left one day, 49
I wanted to marry, but father said, "No—, 56
I went by the Druid stone, 137
*Ice on the Highway*, 176
If but some vengeful god would call to me, 5
If hours be years the twain are blest, 28
"I'll tell—being past all praying for—, 102
*In a Eweleaze near Weatherbury*, 10
In a solitude of the sea, 70
*In Church*, 96

*In Tenebris I*, 38
*In the Cemetery*, 98
*In the Days of Crinoline*, 92
*In the Garden*, 138
*In the Moonlight*, 104
*"In the Night She Came,"* 49
*In the Nuptial Chamber*, 101
*In the Restaurant*, 101
*In the Room of the Bride-Elect*, 97
*In the Small Hours*, 157
*In the Study*, 99
In the third–class seat sat the journeying boy, 136
*In Time of "The Breaking of Nations,"* 141
*Inquiry, The*, 53
It faces west, and round the back and sides, 1
It is August moonlight in the tall plantation, 186
It was at the very date to which we have come, 122
It was your way, my dear, 83
It will be much better when, 170
Its former green is blue and thin, 145


*Jubilate*, 135


Knowing what it bore, 188


Lalage's coming, 112
*Lament*, 84
*Last Chrysanthemum, The*, 32
*Last Love-Word*, 179
*Last Signal, The*, 123
*Last Words to a Dumb Friend*, 162
*Leaving, A*, 188
*Life and Death at Sunrise*, 172
*Logs on the Hearth*,128
*Lonely Days*, 159
Lonely her fate was, 159
Looking forward to the spring, 77
*Lying Awake*, 194

*Mad Judy*, 34

*Man He Killed, The*, 63

*Marble Tablet, The*, 160

*Market-Girl, The*, 52

*Master and the Leaves, The*, 161

*Midnight on the Great Western*, 136

*Missed Train, The*, 182

*Moon Looks In, The*, 91

"My bride is not coming, alas!" says the groom, 100

*"My Spirit Will Not Haunt the Mound,"* 72

My spirit will not haunt the mound, 72

"My stick!" he says, and turns in the lane, 99


*Nature's Questioning*, 9

*Near Lanivet, 1872*, 109

*Neutral Tones*, 5

Never a careworn wife but shows, 29

*Night in November, A*, 150

*Night of the Dance, The*, 50

*No Buyers*, 176

*Nobody Comes*, 180

Nobody took any notice of her as she stood on the causey kerb,
      52

Now I am dead you sing to me, 138


"O lonely workman, standing there, 104

"O 'Melia, my dear, this does everything crown!, 35

"O that mastering tune!" And up in the bed, 101

*Old Furniture*, 126

On afternoons of drowsy calm, 107

*On Sturminster Foot-Bridge*, 126

*On the Death-Bed*, 102

*On the Tune Called the Old-Hundred-and-Fourth*, 151

*One Ralph Blossom Soliloquizes*, 64

*One We Knew*, 61

*One Who Married Above Him*, 177

One without looks in to-night, 150

Only a man harrowing clods, 141

*Orphaned Old Maid, The*, 56

*Outside the Window*, 99
*Over the Coffin*, 103
*Oxen, The*, 120

*Pedigree, The*, 117
Perhaps, long hence, when I have passed away, 6
Pet was never mourned as you, 162
*Photograph, The*, 121
*Poems of 1912–1913*, 79
Portion of this yew, 123
*Procession of Dead Days, A*, 156
*Proud Songsters*, 191

*Rain on a Grave*, 82
Rain on the windows, creaking doors, 48
*Rejected Member's Wife, The*, 46
*Respectable Burgher on "the Higher Criticism," The*, 36
Reticulations creep upon the slack stream's face, 126
Retty used to shake her head, 183
*Retty's Phases*, 183
*Rome: At the Pyramid of Cestius Near the Graves of Shelley and
    Keats*, 21
*Rose-Ann*, 56
*Ruined Maid, The*, 35

*Satires of Circumstance in Fifteen Glimpses*, 96
*Schreckhorn, The*, 75
"See, here's the workbox, little wife, 93
*Self-Unseeing, The*, 37
Seven buxom women abreast, and arm in arm, 176
*Shadow on the Stone, The*, 137
*"She Charged Me,"* 91
She charged me with having said this and that, 91
*She Hears the Storm*, 62
She looked like a bird from a cloud, 108
She looks from the window: still it pours down direly, 194
*She, to Him II*, 6
She told how they used to form for the country dances—, 61
She turned in the high pew, until her sight, 59

*Sheep Fair, A*, 173
*Shortening Days at the Homestead*, 185
*Shut Out That Moon*, 47
Silently I footed by an uphill road, 123
Since Reverend Doctors now declare, 36
Sing, Ballad-singer, raise a hearty tune, 51
"Sixpence a week," says the girl to her lover, 97
*Snow in the Suburbs*, 175
So zestfully canst thou sing?, 114
*"Something Tapped,"* 120
Something tapped on the pane of my room, 120
*Souls of the Slain, The*, 16
*Sundial on a Wet Day, The*, 184
Sweet cyder is a great thing, 124


*Ten Years Since*, 171
That day when oats were reaped, and wheat was ripe, and barley
     ripening, 180
That night your great guns, unawares, 69
The bars are thick with drops that show, 125
The cold moon hangs to the sky by its horn, 50
The day arrives of the autumn fair, 173
The fire advances along the log, 128
The first fire since the summer is lit, and is smoking into the
     room, 185
The flame crept up the portrait line by line, 121
The hills uncap their tops, 172
The kettle descants in a cosy drone, 96
The moving sun-shapes on the spray, 147
The singers are gone from the Cornmarket-place, 54
The sparrow dips in his wheel-rut bath, 130
The sun from the west glares back, 170
The ten hours' light is abating, 78
The thick lids of Night closed upon me, 16
The thrushes sing as the sun is going, 191
The trees are afraid to put forth buds, 133
The two executioners stalk along over the knolls, 193
"The very last time I ever was here," he said, 135
The wind blew words along the skies, 115

The years have gathered grayly, 10

There are some heights in Wessex, shaped as if by a kindly hand, 73

There it stands, though alas, what a little of her, 160

There was a stunted handpost just on the crest, 109

There was a time in former years—, 62

There you are in the dark, 196

There's no more to be done, or feared, or hoped, 60

These flowers are I, poor Fanny Hurd, 152

These market-dames, mid-aged, with lips thin-drawn, 51

They crush together—a rustling heap of flesh—, 129

They sing their dearest songs—, 131

They sit and smoke on the esplanade, 98

They stand confronting, the coffin between, 103

They throw in Drummer Hodge, to rest, 15

Thirty-two years since, up against the sun, 22

This after-sunset is a sight for seeing, 132

This is the weather the cuckoo likes, 145

This the last; the very, very last!, 179

*Thought in Two Moods, A*, 128

Throughout the field I find no grain, 31

*Throwing a Tree*, 193

*Timing Her*, 112

'Tis ten years since, 171

" 'Tis you, I think? Back from your week's work, Steve?", 177

*To an Unborn Pauper Child*, 22

*To Carrey Clavel*, 55

*To Lizbie Browne*, 24

*To My Father's Violin*, 116

*To the Moon*, 111

*Trampwoman's Tragedy, A*, 41

*Transformations*, 123

Tree-leaves labour up and down, 180

*Two-Years' Idyll, A*, 154


*Upbraiding, An*, 138


*Voice, The*, 86

*Voices from Things Growing in a Churchyard*, 152

*Waiting Both*, 169

*Walk, The*, 81

We are budding, Master, budding, 161

We never sang together, 151

*"We Sat at the Window,"* 107

We sat at the window looking out, 107

We shall see her no more, 46

We stood by a pond that winter day, 5

We waited for the sun, 138

*Weathers*, 145

*Wessex Heights*, 73

"What have you looked at, Moon, 111

*When Dead*, 170

When I am in hell or some such place, 64

When I look forth at dawning, pool, 9

When moiling seems at cease, 146

*When Oats Were Reaped*, 180

When the hamlet hailed a birth, 34

When the inmate stirs, the birds retire discreetly, 169

When the Present has latched its postern behind my tremulous
     stay, 142

Where once we danced, where once we sang, 164

*Where They Lived*, 119

*"Who's in the Next Room?"*, 133

"Who's in the next room?—who?, 133

Who, then, was Cestius, 21

Why did you give no hint that night, 79

Why didn't you say you was promised, Rose-Ann?, 56

Why should this flower delay so long, 32

*Wife Waits, A*, 54

Will's at the dance in the Club-room below, 54

William Dewy, Tranter Reuben, Farmer Ledlow late at plough,
     7

*"Wind Blew Words, The,"* 115

*Winter in Durnover Field*, 31

Wintertime nighs, 38

Within a churchyard, on a recent grave,
     129

*Without Ceremony*, 83

*Wives in the Sere*, 29

Woman much missed, how you call to me, call to me, 86

*Workbox, The*, 93

"Would it had been the man of our wish!", 97

Yes; such it was, 154

You did not walk with me, 81

You may have seen, in road or street, 174

You, Morningtide Star, now are steady-eyed, over the east, 194

"You see those mothers squabbling there?", 98

You turn your back, you turn your back, 55

*Your Last Drive*, 80

*Zermatt: To the Matterhorn*, 22

# FOR THE BEST IN PAPERBACKS, LOOK FOR THE

In every corner of the world, on every subject under the sun, Penguin represents quality and variety—the very best in publishing today.

For complete information about books available from Penguin—including Penguin Classics, Penguin Compass, and Puffins—and how to order them, write to us at the appropriate address below. Please note that for copyright reasons the selection of books varies from country to country.

**In the United States:** Please write to *Penguin Group (USA), P.O. Box 12289 Dept. B, Newark, New Jersey 07101-5289* or call 1-800-788-6262.

**In the United Kingdom:** Please write to *Dept. EP, Penguin Books Ltd, Bath Road, Harmondsworth, West Drayton, Middlesex UB7 0DA.*

**In Canada:** Please write to *Penguin Books Canada Ltd, 90 Eglinton Avenue East, Suite 700, Toronto, Ontario M4P 2Y3.*

**In Australia:** Please write to *Penguin Books Australia Ltd, P.O. Box 257, Ringwood, Victoria 3134.*

**In New Zealand:** Please write to *Penguin Books (NZ) Ltd, Private Bag 102902, North Shore Mail Centre, Auckland 10.*

**In India:** Please write to *Penguin Books India Pvt Ltd, 11 Panchsheel Shopping Centre, Panchsheel Park, New Delhi 110 017.*

**In the Netherlands:** Please write to *Penguin Books Netherlands bv, Postbus 3507, NL-1001 AH Amsterdam.*

**In Germany:** Please write to *Penguin Books Deutschland GmbH, Metzlerstrasse 26, 60594 Frankfurt am Main.*

**In Spain:** Please write to *Penguin Books S. A., Bravo Murillo 19, 1° B, 28015 Madrid.*

**In Italy:** Please write to *Penguin Italia s.r.l., Via Benedetto Croce 2, 20094 Corsico, Milano.*

**In France:** Please write to *Penguin France, Le Carré Wilson, 62 rue Benjamin Baillaud, 31500 Toulouse.*

**In Japan:** Please write to *Penguin Books Japan Ltd, Kaneko Building, 2-3-25 Koraku, Bunkyo-Ku, Tokyo 112.*

**In South Africa:** Please write to *Penguin Books South Africa (Pty) Ltd, Private Bag X14, Parkview, 2122 Johannesburg.*